best of residential

INTERIOR DESIGN BEST OF RESIDENTIAL

EDITOR IN CHIEF
Cindy Allen

EXECUTIVE EDITOR
Jen Renzi

SENIOR DESIGNER
Karla Lima

DESIGNERS
Selena Chen
Zigeng Li

PREPRESS IMAGING SPECIALIST
Igor Tsiperson

PRODUCTION
Sarah Dentry

EDITORS
Kathryn Daniels
Stephen Treffinger

BOOKS DIRECTOR
Kathy Harrigan

MANAGING EDITOR
Helene E. Oberman

PRODUCTION MANAGER
Christopher Havel

CONTRIBUTING WRITERS
Liz Arnold
Jesse Dorris
Jennifer Krichels Gorsche
Monica Khemsurov
Georgina McWhirter
Annette Rose-Shapiro
David Sokol
Athena Waligore

MARKETING DIRECTOR
Tina Brennan

MARKETING ART DIRECTOR
Denise Figueroa

Library of Congress Control Number 2012930896
ISBN-10: 0-9833263-3-9
ISBN-13: 978-0-9833263-3-5
Printed in China
10 9 8 7 6 5 4 3 2 1

INTERIOR
DESIGN®

INTERIOR DESIGN MAGAZINE
360 Park Avenue South, 17th Floor, New York, NY 10010
www.interiordesign.net

SANDOW
Brands Powered by Innovation

SANDOW MEDIA LLC
Corporate Headquarters
3651 NW 8th Avenue, Boca Raton, FL 33431
www.sandowmedia.com

SANDOW, publisher of NewBeauty®, Worth®, Luxe Interiors + Design™, Watch
Journal®, Furniture/Today® Group, and Interior Design®, is a leader in building
multi-platform brands that inform, inspire, and engage highly coveted consumer
and business audiences. Meeting at the intersection of luxury and design, the
SANDOW brands—all powered by innovation—span digital and print media,
licensing, consulting, e-commerce and retail, business information and marketing services. Learn more at sandow.com.

foreword
by Cindy Allen

There's no place like home. There *is* no place like home. There's no place...You get the drift.

Never has that wizardly saying rung more true, when you consider the chaos of our hustle-and-bustle, tech-driven lives.

Home has become the ultimate sanctuary. It's our refuge, our getaway to escape the world—or engage in it full-on. And we're definitely not in Kansas anymore. We traveled the world from Minnesota to Monte Carlo, from Hawaii to Kuwait, and back again.

I'm delighted to present *Interior Design Best of Residential*, the newest book in our growing series (*Best of Year*, *Best of Hospitality*, and *Best of Office* preceded). You'll see in the following pages what boundless imagination and enormous commitment can accomplish.

Who stands behind all this vision and talent? According to our 2010 Universe study, there are more than 25,000 design firms in the United States, and 52 percent of them handle residential projects. That translates to a whopping 26,000 individual designers potentially working on your home! The scale of the firms—from small studios with fewer than five designers to businesses employing 20 or more—may vary, but the results in this book are uniformly s-t-e-l-l-a-r.

The money involved is nothing to sneeze at, either. Consider this: Among residential design firms, the average home is valued at $2.3 million, and designers specify nearly $1.8 million in products a year. And we can't talk about the home without celebrating its heart, the kitchen, and everyone's favorite private oasis, the bath. Clients clearly agree, putting their money where their mouth is: The average kitchen renovation costs $86,000 and a bathroom, $47,000.

If you're interested in today's trends, we've made it easy for you. The book is divided into eight chapters we think defines them: Inside/Outside, Vintage Modern, City Living, Modern Family, Getaways, Green, New Tradition, and Global Inspiration. Prepare to be dazzled...and inspired. Just tap your heels three times and you'll be there.

best of residential
contents

best of residential
contents

MAYA ROMANOFF.COM · *extraordinary surfacing materials* · MOTHER OF PEARL MARQUETRY™ TILES OF GENUINE SEASHELL

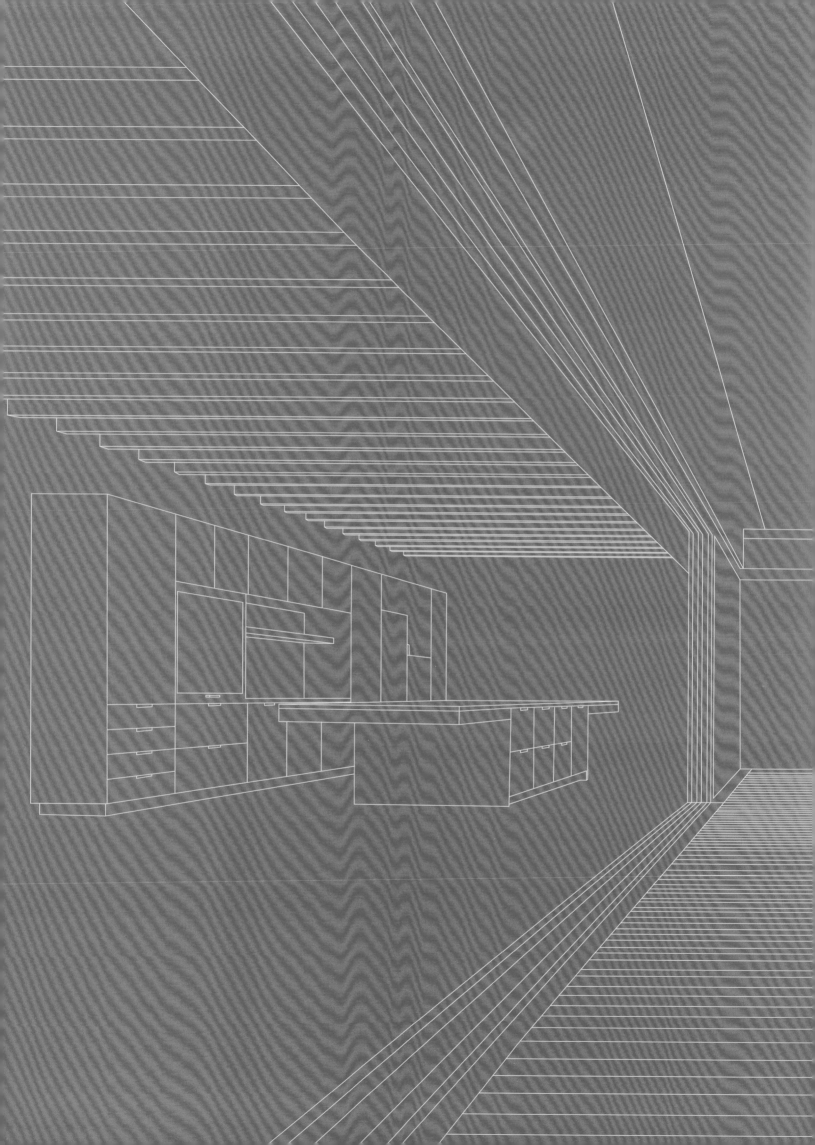

inside/outside

The residents of Rio, Los Angeles, and other temperate climes don't have a lock on indoor/outdoor living (though they surely have an edge).

As evidenced herein, even Northeasterners want a piece of the action. After all, when warm weather is fleeting, you want to take in as much as you can—and embrace sunlight and panoramic vistas all year long. The tool kit: full-height windows that frame specific views like works of art, plein-air soaking tubs, paradisiacal courtyards, luminous skylights, and sliding-glass walls—or (why not?) no walls at all. Since even Southern California gets chilly, patio fireplaces, insulated glazing, and radiant heating are a must. *Feel the breeze.*

Belzberg Architects and MLK Studio

TORONTO RESIDENCE

The clients of this suburban Toronto stunner contacted Hagy Belzberg wanting a design similar to another of his they'd spotted in a magazine—on the outside, that is. While admiring the straight lines and indoor/outdoor features of the original, which skewed very Cali modern, they sought a more casual home that spoke to their South African roots.

Belzberg, working in collaboration with interior designer Meg Joannides, responded with a rough-hewn aesthetic and open-plan living areas delineated by ceiling height. A staircase with a wavy, CNC-carved walnut screen forms a sculptural centerpiece; details—such as variable-width walnut flooring with a hand-scraped finish—imbue the interiors with an African game park–like feel.

Those organic touches accomplished a dual objective: They added an extra layer of warmth to a home that, owing to its northern location, is inclined to invite in not just summer but a long, long winter as well. Climate was an impetus, too, in installing insulated glazing and radiant subfloor heating throughout.

The design was driven largely by a desire to take advantage of surrounding views. Most rooms have adjoining balconies, and a window wall frames the wide swath of trees that line the ravine out back. Courtesy of the ever changing panorama, the vibe within may vary by season, but there's one constant: The dead of winter and heart of summer are equally dramatic.

"Transferring the indoor/outdoor concept from L.A. to Toronto was our main challenge"

—HAGY BELZBERG

Clockwise from above: The stair's angled walnut fins. Upstairs, the glass-enclosed walkway leading to the master bedroom features an abstracted zebra-print runner and an African artwork, both nods to the clients' heritage. A bank of retractable-glass doors allow for a seamless indoor/outdoor transition. The shapely exterior is detailed with zinc fasciae. ⮞

9,000 sf
5 bedrooms, 7 ½ bathrooms

0 10 20 40

1 ENTRY

2 OFFICE

3 LIVING AREA

4 SITTING AREA

5 TERRACE

6 KITCHEN

7 DINING AREA

8 GARAGE

Clockwise from above: *The main-floor terrace provides a roof for the lower level, which houses a media room and gym. The living area features a 12-foot-long custom recessed bookshelf for showcasing collectibles; the stacked-limestone motif continues with the fireplace tower. Bordering the dining room is a stacked-limestone wall that extends the facade, visually uniting interior and exterior while contrasting with wood finishes. The master suite's 16-foot custom leather headboard and a brass-strip sculpture by Dennis Lin anchor a king-size bed. In the marble-clad master bath, a solar shade offers privacy when needed.*

PROJECT TEAM HAGY BELZBERG, DAN RENTSCH, CORY TAYLOR, BROCK DESMIT,
CHRIS ARNTZEN, DAVID CHEUNG, BARRY GARTIN, ASHLEY COON
INTERIOR DESIGN MEG JOANNIDES/MLK STUDIO
PHOTOGRAPHY BEN RAHN/A-FRAME

www.belzbergarchitects.com

www.mlkstudio.com

Dirk Denison Architects

Hired to build a single-story home and a guesthouse for a family of four, Dirk Denison made his first order of business a survey of the view—or, rather, the lack of a primary one. The site was walled in by a stand of mature redwoods on one side and a mountain range on the other. So Denison looked within, so to speak, creating *interior* views instead by weaving courtyards and gardens through a "village" of glass-enclosed structures. The result is a home with as many outdoor as indoor rooms.

Steel-and-glass circulation spines knit together the complex, which is bound by a cedar-shingled perimeter wall. For the gardens, Denison eschewed flowers and ornate foliage, adhering to a spare yet architectural palette of olive trees, Japanese maples, bamboo, rushes, and redwoods.

The floor plan is based on an irregular grid, a pattern that informs decorative elements as well, from the family room's faceted limestone fireplace to the nested rectangles that compose the custom headboard in the master suite. Ceiling planes are subtly fractured and folded, peeling up here and there to reveal skylights. The abundance of glass coaxes natural light into the structure in a sculptural manner. Despite the transparency, Denison ensured that privacy is a nonissue: Each bathroom, for instance, overlooks its own courtyard, rendering curtains unnecessary.

Clockwise from above: A long walkway between pavilions terminates at the entryway, positioned at the center of the complex. Threaded through the floor plan are eight landscaped courtyards. An oversize vessel by Archie Held anchors a reflecting pool in the central courtyard. ➤

1 ENTRY

2 MASTER SUITE

3 LIVING/DINING ROOM

4 KITCHEN

5 OUTDOOR DINING

6 FAMILY ROOM

7 BEDROOM

8 PLAYROOM

0 10 20   40

Clockwise from above: In the living room, a custom sofa—based on a Christian Liaigre chair—faces two Michael Berman club chairs and a Richard Meier coffee table. Bamboo and rushes accent a courtyard. A Harry Bertoia sculpture echoes the I-beams that frame the building. Denison designed the bed and headboard; Holly Hunt night tables join a custom alpaca rug from De Sousa Hughes. A custom limestone sink and tub furnish the master bath. Executive chairs by Eero Saarinen surround a custom dining table.

7,100 sf
1 ½-acre site

PROJECT TEAM DIRK DENISON, ANDREA COCHRAN, LAURA BLUMENFELD
BUILDER REDHORSE CONSTRUCTORS
PHOTOGRAPHY JOSHUA McHUGH
www.dirkdenisonarchitects.com

Clockwise from below: *The property is part of a 19th-century planned residential community adjacent to a common park. In the skylit entry, a stair leads to the lower level; the living room opens to the right. A slim window filters light from the gravel entry court into the garage. Bluestone surrounds the lap pool on the lower level. White cedar warms the exterior's brick and stucco cladding. A view past the dining room and toward the windowed breakfast nook exemplifies the design's emphasis on sight lines.*

Austerity and warmth meet on the same plane in a house built for single-level living. The clients, a retired couple, envisioned a modern and inviting residence of modest scale in which to exhibit their art and furniture collections. Architect Deborah Berke executed a serene space with gallerylike white walls softened by floors and paneling rendered in welcoming bamboo. A skylight and massive windows coax the outdoors in; sun exposure and specific trees on the verdant property informed the fenestration and spatial organization.

Attentive balance extends to the exterior as well, where stucco is tempered by weathered cedar and pewter-gray brick whose natural texture looks handcrafted. Berke conceived the materials palette as a composition of varied but complementary finishes, detailed to express their methods of construction; as in a black-and-white photograph, the tonal similarities create visual unity.

Using the sloping site to her advantage, Berke grouped the main spaces on the entry level, including several multifunctional areas that serve as guest rooms or offices. Down a short staircase walled in waist-high glass, a lap pool and a flex room enjoy expansive views. With the clients' long-term needs in mind, all rooms are wheelchair accessible, and the stair is wide enough for a lift.

Deborah Berke Partners

TULIP AVENUE, LLEWELLYN PARK
WEST ORANGE, NEW JERSEY

5,400 sf
3 bedrooms, 3 ½ bathrooms

PROJECT TEAM DEBORAH BERKE, MARC LEFF, AMEET HIREMATH, STEPHANIE LAM
LANDSCAPE ARCHITECT ZION BREEN & RICHARDSON ASSOCIATES
STRUCTURAL ENGINEER ROSS DALLAND
CIVIL ENGINEER LEHR ASSOCIATES
GENERAL CONTRACTOR DRILL CONSTRUCTION
PHOTOGRAPHY JASON SCHMIDT

www.dberke.com

Dirk Denison
Architects

PRIVATE RESIDENCE
CARMEL-BY-THE-SEA, CALIFORNIA

An Tearmann is an Irish term for sanctuary, and for a house so named, Dirk Denison was tapped to achieve refuge without breaching the town's stringent building restrictions. In a top-to-bottom renovation, the Chicago modernist channeled regional Midcentury architecture and historic Japanese design to create calm in small quarters.

Although the property overlooks Carmel Bay and the Pacific Ocean, Denison devised an inward-facing solution that minimized exterior modifications and created seclusion in a dense neighborhood. Reusing the existing foundation, he configured living spaces around a rectangular central courtyard. Above it, a glass roof thwarts salt air while preserving the connection to the elements; teak daybeds and an *ofuro* soaking tub set on river stones enhance the outdoorsy spirit. This sunlit core is visible from the office, galley kitchen, and dinette through vertical mahogany screens that read as opaque when viewed from an angle. The living room and master suite open directly onto the courtyard via folding walls that can be shut when more privacy is desired.

Solar thermal gain through the glass roof creates little call for mechanical heating; the clients rarely have to use their radiant flooring. There's no need for AC either: Opening a few exterior windows can flush the rooms with cool air. The second floor takes advantage of natural ventilation as well. An oculus-topped meditation room opens to a pair of porches surveying the peaceful horizon.

Clockwise from above: *In the upstairs meditation room, a tatami mat hides a sunken mattress that lies flush with the teak floor. The narrow entry path traces the long southern elevation of the interior courtyard. A built-in custom dining banquette in mahogany marks the northwest corner of the house; the CH20 chairs are by Hans Wegner. The quiet stack of cedar-clad volumes belies the interior's full complexity. With folding walls open, the living room offers views of the courtyard and the master suite beyond from an Eames lounge or a rocking chair by Mira Nakashima.* ⤳

1,950 sf
2 bedrooms, 2 bathrooms

0   5   10   20

1 ENTRY

2 LIVING ROOM

3 PORCH

4 DINING AREA

5 KITCHEN

6 OFFICE

7 MASTER SUITE

8 COURTYARD

PHOTOGRAPHY DAVID MATHESON

www.dirkdenisonarchitects.com

Clockwise from top: Eames and Nakashima are paired again in the office, which surveys the courtyard through a slatted wall alternating columns and posts. Toward the rear of the courtyard, an ofuro soaking tub enjoys celestial views. A handwoven ombré runner accents the kitchen's mahogany cabinets, topped in Midnight granite. The sight line from the kitchen to the living room demonstrates the true porosity of the variable-height vertical screen.

Standard

HIDDEN HOUSE, LOS ANGELES

Starting from scratch isn't always the best way to innovate. Take this Glassell Park property: Standard was originally commissioned to scrap the existing 1940s structure and build a ground-up home for the family who had purchased it. But the architects realized it would be advantageous— environmentally and code-wise, for starters—to integrate the existing two-bedroom into the new design. That revelation proved key to the project's success.

Standard converted the old volume into a living/dining area and added a kitchen, family room, office, garage, master suite, and more to effectively double the square footage. Pivot and pocket doors dissolve boundaries between living quarters and adjacent courtyards and patios, allowing for a seamless indoor/outdoor experience. Cork and reclaimed end-grain wood—along with high-efficiency appliances—were selected for their ecofriendliness (as was the sustainable cotton insulation).

Located at the end of a half-mile unpaved road, the house sits on a lushly landscaped site. The new plantings— oak, sycamore, manzanita—transition comfortably to native chaparral. There are kitchen gardens, organic flower beds, and a chicken coop. Even though the property can see to downtown Los Angeles, it feels a world apart.

PROJECT TEAM JEFFREY ALLSBROOK, SILVIA KUHLE
PHOTOGRAPHY BENNY CHAN/FOTOWORKS

www.standard-la.com

Clockwise from left:
*The house unfolds
around a courtyard;
the kitchen's pocket
door spans 24 feet.
The living/dining area
is bracketed by pivot
doors that open to the
patio and courtyard,
creating a de facto
breezeway. New
plantings mesh with
the surrounding scrub
and kitchen gardens.
Redwood details and
cement plaster walls
unify the old and
new construction.*

3,500 sf
7-acre site
Remodel + addition

16,000 sf
3 bedrooms, 6 bathrooms

Gisele Taranto Arquitetura

TEMPO HOUSE, RIO DE JANEIRO, BRAZIL

This Spanish colonial–style house had much to offer. Located in one of Rio's most charming neighborhoods, the property was master-planned by famed Brazilian landscape architect Roberto Burle Marx and included a second structure housing staff quarters, a theater, and a spa. But the clients desired an aesthetic update, greater contact with the verdant surroundings, and a more free-flowing layout befitting their lifestyle.

Gisele Taranto preserved the original footprint but demolished interior walls and tiled roofs to rework the floor plan. A third story was added to each structure—an office and roof garden on the main house and a two-bedroom apartment on the staff wing—to embrace views of nearby mountains. Enlarged windows and doors framed in aluminum forge a strong indoor/outdoor connection while canopies offer protection from strong rain and harsh sunlight. The white-walled foyer—accessed via a 20-foot-high entry door—was converted into an art gallery.

Luxe but quiet finishes take a backseat to the artwork: *peroba do campo* wood, statuary marble, Bateig Blue limestone, and Cor-Ten steel. The latter clads the stair, powder room walls, and the pergola spanning the living room. These weightier elements are leavened with glass ceilings and the warm wood tones of plush Italian and Brazilian furnishings. Adding to the airy vibe are resplendent sweeps of exotic flora and the year-round circulation of tropical breezes.

Clockwise from top left: An installation by Brazilian artist Cildo Meireles hangs in the double-height entry gallery. At the base of a wood-slat screen, a pergola in Cor-Ten steel lends a contemporary edge to the indoor/outdoor living area. A work by Mira Schendel presides over the dining room, lit by Skygarden pendants. The living room opens onto a lush outdoor seating area, where pairs of Paola Lenti armchairs square off beneath the pergola. ➤

Clockwise from top left: The property features a pool as well as landscaping by the late Burle Marx (with an update from Gilberto Elkis). The palette of Bateig Blue limestone, Cor-Ten steel, and aluminum established in the main house continues in the spa. The library features built-in shelving by CAP Marcenarias and swiveling leather armchairs by Vico Magistretti. An Up5 chair and footstool by Gaetano Pesce animate the top floor's stark office. Straw wall covering instills warmth in the master bedroom.

1 ENTRY GALLERY

2 LIVING ROOM

3 DINING ROOM

4 LIBRARY

5 STAIR

6 KITCHEN

7 THEATER

8 GARAGE

9 POOL

0 10 20   40

DESIGN PRINCIPAL GISELE TARANTO
WOOD SHADES, CARPENTRY SETE & ARTE PORTAS E JANELAS
FURNITURE CASUAL INTERIORES
WOOD FURNITURE CAP MARCENARIAS
ELECTRIC, AUTOMATION, SECURITY, AND COMMUNICATION ENGINEERING ENDEV
PHOTOGRAPHY MCA ESTUDIO

www.giseletaranto.com

Philpotts Interiors

INTERNATIONAL STYLE
KOHALA COAST, HAWAII

Designed by San Francisco architect Shay Zak with interiors by Mary Philpotts McGrath, this oceanfront dwelling on the island's Kohala Coast is not your average family home. It was built in the style of a Hawaiian village, with a dozen-plus pavilions dotting the rolling lawns. Each Pacific Asian–inspired structure is devoted to a different program: There's a master suite, a dining pavilion, guest living and bedroom spaces, a place for the children, and a hub for recreation. The structures appear elemental, with huge wood beams that promise to last forever and roofs that soar above an open framework.

The task of Philpotts McGrath was to draw these separate elements into a cohesive whole; the parts needed to "speak to each other," as the designer puts it. To achieve this, she complemented the deep wood structures with furnishings in reclaimed ipe, teak, and native koa. Antique fish-trap baskets retrofitted with bulbs to create pendant lights are a unique, locally inspired hallmark. At night, outer pathways are lit in an almost sculptural manner, drawing you in to the surroundings, and a fire bowl marks a pool overlooking the Pacific, neatly echoing the Hualalai volcano in the distance.

The end result? An elegantly designed home that embodies resort chic, creates a seamless indoor/outdoor experience, and is as captivating at night as it is by day.

Clockwise from above: Stone walls lend texture and a sense of comforting solidity. The main pavilion frames a view of the entrance courtyard; Philpotts McGrath used found wood for custom tables and tabletops throughout. The house glows like a jewel in the dark: Flickering torches dot the grounds and small spotlights embedded in pavilion ceilings add drama to the open structures. The master bedroom's custom koa bed was designed to allow for ocean views—even from a prone position. A verdant walkway between pavilions. ➘

16,023 sf interior
22,000 sf lot
11 bedrooms, 12 bathrooms,
3 half bathrooms

Clockwise from top:
The TV/billiard pavilion
surveys the palm
courtyard. One of two
pools, lit from within,
makes a statement
with its bronze fire
bowl from India.
The open-air dining
pavilion features a
teak table and chairs
by Summit. The
master bedroom
vanity is topped with
Beluga granite and
fossil travertine.

0 20 40 80

1 ENTRY PAVILION
2 SPORT COURTS
3 KIDS' COTTAGE
4 MASTER COTTAGE
5 MAIN RESIDENCE
6 POOL
7 DINING HUT
8 FAMILY PAVILION
9 GUEST COTTAGE
10 GUEST PAVILION
11 GARAGE

DESIGN PRINCIPAL MARY PHILPOTTS McGRATH
ARCHITECT OF RECORD ZAK ARCHITECTURE
LANDSCAPE ARCHITECT SUZMAN & COLE DESIGN ASSOCIATES
PHOTOGRAPHY MATTHEW MILLMAN

www.philpotts.net

vintage modern

"Something old, something new" isn't just for brides. Vintage charm mixed with modern-day spirit is coveted in the residential realm, too.

A favored strategy of design aficionados is to riff off a home's period details—often reestablished or refurbished—with a more of-the-moment decor: heavy on clean, bold lines, tempered with a touch of minimalism. Wedded to no one era, these residences, which range from a Brooklyn brownstone to a Manhattan Beach aerie, are all about stylistic fusion. Midcentury-modern furniture cohabits blissfully with contemporary art and classic *objets* from the 1930s. *It's all in the mix.*

Robert Kaner Interior Design

FOREST HILLS RESIDENCE, QUEENS, NEW YORK

Shortly after inaugurating the Russell Sage Foundation in 1907 to improve living conditions in the United States, Margaret Olivia Slocum Sage decided to perform her own experiment in the field. She commissioned society architect Grosvenor Atterbury and landscape scion Frederick Law Olmsted Jr. to develop 142 acres of outer-borough New York according to City Beautiful principles. This alternative to industrial-era housing yielded spacious revivalist manses overlooking lush streetscapes, and today a private review board protects those original design standards.

A real-estate developer and a photojournalist presented Robert Kaner with an analogous task in renovating a neighborhood home for them and their twin daughters: to give the formal interior a more contemporary sensibility and livable configuration—while respecting the Georgian-style house's extant features. Working within the historic building envelope, Kaner enhanced the sense of openness by replacing the downstairs eating nook, powder room, mudroom, and foyer with a more simple, bifurcated kitchen and serving area. And on the second floor, he consolidated a half bath and closet to make a new master bathroom.

With a few stunning exceptions—such as the dining room that pulsates in deep red and the bathrooms completed in bold monochromes like cobalt and celadon—neutral colors stress continuity between spaces. The soft palette also draws the eye to moldings and other 1930s ornamentation. Very apropos.

Clockwise from right: In the living room, a Serpentine sofa by Vladimir Kagan faces a sleek honed-limestone fireplace that replaced the original faux Chippendale design. Pratt & Lambert Velvet Red envelops the dining room, which is illuminated by a Glow chandelier. A bench by Brendon Farrell provides a modernist counterpoint to the traditional foyer. The client, a family of four, moved from a Manhattan loft to this Georgian Revival house. ➤

Clockwise from opposite: In the living room, contemporary art cohabitates with period paneling. Because the antiquated kitchen was not suitable for modern family living, the client gave Kaner free rein in renovating it; he installed cherry cabinetry by Effeti, stainless-steel appliances, and a multicolor glass-tile backsplash. In the entry hall, a combination of neutral wall colors and dark-stained flooring effects a cozy atmosphere and puts the focus on 1930s-era architectural details. Kaner regularly designs furniture for his projects, such as the master bedroom's storage units.

DESIGN PRINCIPAL ROBERT KANER
PHOTOGRAPHY TOM POWEL (1, 3–8); ANNIE SCHLECHTER (2)
www.kanerid.com

4,700 sf
6 bedrooms,
5 ½ bathrooms

0   10   20   40

1 ENTRANCE HALL

2 DINING ROOM

3 PLAYROOM

4 CASUAL DINING AREA

5 DEN

6 KITCHEN

7 LIVING ROOM

8 LIBRARY

2,600 sf
3 bedroom, 3½ baths

Dufner Heighes

LAKE MICHIGAN GUESTHOUSE
NORTHERN MICHIGAN

Clockwise from above: *Dufner Heighes replaced the existing fenestration with handcrafted steel windows and doors; the home is heated by a ground-source pump with geothermal wells. In the living room— kitted out with an alpaca rug and seating by Jens Risom and Jean-Michel Frank— the wood-clad ceiling echoes the hearth's graphic stonework. A vintage carved-ironwood bird perches on a rosewood-top Saarinen Tulip table in a guest bedroom. A Tom Dixon pendant illuminates the breakfast nook, furnished with a trestle table and custom banquette. A Brad Phillips painting hangs in the foyer, above a Børge Mogensen sofa and a botanical rug.* ➤

Sometimes you want peace and solitude on a vacation; other times, you want a lively crowd. The latter was true for the firm's longtime clients—a couple with four kids—who desired to convert a 1940s cottage beside their Lake Michigan summer home into a guesthouse.

The space had a great aura. Partners Gregory Dufner and Daniel Heighes Wismer endeavored to keep it by rebuilding the structure from the inside. They excavated the floors to increase the ceiling height without disturbing the charming, undulating, moss-covered roof. (The original plastic-panel ceiling was switched out for a new design in wood.) The designers left intact the fireplace's spectacular stonework and sourced additional stone from the same local quarry to replace wall-to-wall carpeting. The existing floor plan shifted only slightly, to accommodate a larger master suite and a relocated front door.

Outside, the duo extended the stone terrace even closer to the waterfront to better utilize the house's prime location and maximize outdoor living space. Inside, they filled the cottage with a variety of antique finds as well as contemporary pieces inspired by Midcentury classics.

And while the cottage serves as a getaway, the project was no holiday for Dufner Heighes. The owners acquired it in the fall and wanted it ready for the following Fourth of July. Everything was finished in time for the fireworks; the house filled up with guests, and the festivities commenced.

6,000 sf
5 bedrooms,
6½ bathrooms

1 ENTRY

2 MASTER SUITE

3 POOL

4 PING-PONG TABLE

5 PATIO

6 MEDIA ROOM

7 BATHROOM

8 BEDROOM

9 OFFICE

0   10   20   40

Clockwise from left: *The facade of the Brooklyn brownstone. In the stairwell, a Wohlert pendant lamp by Louis Poulsen illuminates rift-cut, quartered white-oak floors. Eames chairs flank the custom dining table. The living room is furnished with vintage armchairs, a custom couch, '60s table lamps, and a table by Ochre; the vintage chandeliers throughout were found in Hudson, New York.*

Steven Harris Architects

MONTAGUE TERRACE, BROOKLYN, NEW YORK

Before Remodelista cofounder Francesca Connolly and her family could inhabit their brownstone on a historic block in Brooklyn Heights, a gut renovation was required. The 27-foot-wide building, briefly occupied by Thomas Wolfe in the 1930s, had been divided into a warren of apartments in the '70s. In reunifying the townhouse, architect Steven Harris modified the layout only slightly—the kitchen was relocated, for instance—and honored the rooms' original proportions. Some period details were rehabbed, while others were upgraded to contemporary standards. One obvious modification is the dining room windows, which were replaced with custom steel frames.

The decor, a collaboration with Lucien Rees Roberts, beautifully complements the refurbished spaces. Scale was a primary driver of the design, especially with respect to custom pieces: Just the right balance needed to be struck so that the rooms seemed neither spare nor overwrought. A mix of iconic Midcentury pieces plays against more traditional details—such as the ornate mantels in the living room—while a muted palette for carpets and fabrics heightens the sculptural presence of the furnishings. The clever hybrid dining table, a custom top on a vintage Florence Knoll base, epitomizes the amalgamation of old and new. And though the interiors have been left exceptionally open, with plenty of breathing room, they still manage to feel cozy and inviting.

6,250 sf
5 bedrooms,
6 ½ bathrooms

Clockwise from top left: *The custom kitchen cabinets are made of Corian. A minimalist custom shower stall in the master bathroom. A Castiglioni pendant and sconces by Best Lighting join a custom chaise and bed; the floor lamp is by David Weeks. A salvaged plastic chandelier, vintage loveseat (covered in an Osborne & Little floral), and Pierre Paulin chair furnish the daughter's bedroom. The son's bedroom features an IQ pendant lamp and Warren Platner lounge chair. The sitting room, with a David Weeks mobile pendant, a B&B Italia couch, and an Amoeba table by T. H. Robsjohn Gibbings.*

DESIGN TEAM STEVEN HARRIS, BILL GREAVES, TOWFIQ AWWAL, ELIZABETH BACON
INTERIOR DESIGN LUCIEN REES ROBERTS/REES ROBERTS + PARTNERS
PHOTOGRAPHY SCOTT FRANCES/OTTO

www.stevenharrisarchitects.com

Charles M. Rabinovitch Architects

ARCHITECT'S RESIDENCE, RIVERDALE, NEW YORK

A pergola is not something you expect to encounter at a residence within New York City limits. But this formerly plain redbrick facade in the verdant Bronx enclave of Riverdale indeed features one. A composition of ipe and stainless steel, the sleek latticework structure is as airy, modern, and welcoming as the house itself.

It wasn't always so. When architect Charles Rabinovitch set out to design a new home for his family—his artist wife

and the couple's three children—that also encompassed a work space for himself, the 1954 residence presented numerous challenges. In particular, the cramped and dark interior cried out for a major transformation. Rabinovitch started by replacing walls—and some floors—with glass, and installed skylights and overhead transoms. The architect also swapped multi-pane windows for larger bay-style "boxes" that project outward to catch light. These modifications allowed him to capitalize on one of the house's greatest assets: the wooded lot it stands on.

Now the home is an open, bright aerie, each window revealing a leafy view. The distinction between interior and exterior has been blurred; it's not always easy to tell where the house ends and the landscape begins. Which is precisely what Rabinovitch had in mind.

Clockwise from above: Visitors approach the house from the pergola side; the former garage, tucked behind the etched-glass door, was reincarnated as a work and exercise room. The typeface of the house numbers hints at the home's vernacular. The owner's Midcentury-modern clock collection provides a whimsical focal point. Soothing neutrals prevail in a bedroom. Another collection, of pottery from the same era, fills an alcove above the entry gallery. ➤

Clockwise from top left: A perforated divider screens the staircase from the lower-level office. Eaves, a skylight, and unobtrusive storage give a child's bedroom a cozy garret—like feel. Living room furnishings continue the Midcentury-modern vein. Niches housing more of the family's pottery collection flank the wide top-floor landing. The architect combined a series of small utility spaces to create the kitchen, featuring Jerusalem stone flooring, mosaic-clad walls, and color-washed white-oak cabinetry.

2,600 sf
3 levels
2-year renovation

PROJECT TEAM CHARLES M. RABINOVITCH, ANDREA RABINOVITCH
PHOTOGRAPHY ANDREA BRIZZI
www.archrabin.com

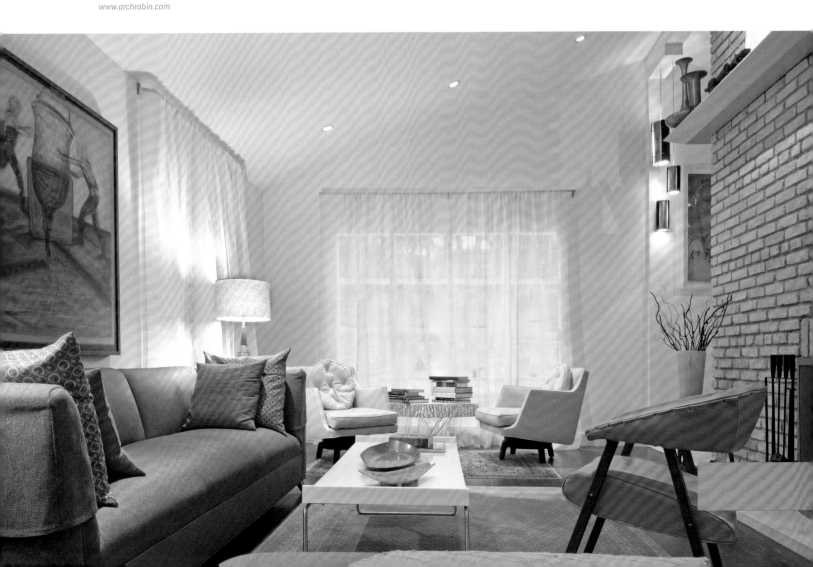

3,300 sf
4 bedrooms, 3 bathrooms

Studio19 Architects

MERCER RESIDENCE, SEATTLE

Having your own home scrutinized is an occupational hazard when you're an architect. Trickier than opening your doors for all to see, though, is living in a space that's entirely closed off from views, a lesson Studio19 Architects principal Hui Tian learned upon finding her dream home. Sight lines—not to mention stunning lake vistas through the living room's wraparound picture windows—were blocked by a warren of wood-paneled rooms and a front hall that led straight to the staircase. Keeping intact the Midcentury envelope, Tian gutted the interior, doing away with nearly every division in the living areas.

First to go was the staircase leading to the basement, which was relocated behind a door next to the kitchen. With the entry closet demolished as well, guests stepping through the front door now have an unobstructed view of the kitchen, dining, and living areas. Tian underscored the feeling of lightness with a subtle cantilever motif that distinguishes the coffee table, sofa, and kitchen counter. The only wall left in place (for structural reasons) now sections off a reading nook flanked by a triple-sided transparent fireplace, where Tian and her husband retreat when they want a snug alternative to the newfound expansiveness. After all, architects—even those unafraid to flaunt their handiwork—sometimes need privacy, too.

Clockwise from right: Exposed during the wall demolition, awkward ceiling angles created by past additions were drywalled over to soften the visual impact. Floors are fumed white oak; cabinetry is wenge. A triple-sided gas fireplace warms the living room and the adjacent reading nook, both overlooking the lake. The only remaining divisions are those bordering the bathroom and bedrooms lining the hall near the entry. ➤

1 ENTRY

2 LIVING AREA

3 READING NOOK

4 DINING AREA

5 KITCHEN

6 BEDROOM

7 MASTER SUITE

0   10   20   40

DESIGN PRINCIPAL HUI TIAN, AIA, MAIBC, LEED AP
PHOTOGRAPHY MING-YI HSU
www.studio19architects.com

Clockwise from near left: A nod to Eastern living appears in the master bathroom, where a tiled foot-soaking tub is tucked behind the bathtub. In the master bedroom, a backlit drywall "headboard" adds ambience, while the radiant-heated floors are warp-resistant engineered hardwood. A frameless glass shower enclosure and recessed medicine cabinet make the guest bathroom feel more spacious. Though the guest bedroom shrunk a bit when the new basement stair was installed behind it, it now features hotel-style lightswitches on either side of the bed. A Gregg pendant in satinized glass adds a focal point—and a sense of drama— to the dining area.

The Egg Design Group

MANOR HOUSE, BAYSIDE, WISCONSIN

Those who discover this Milwaukee suburb are likely to call it home for generations. One house near the shores of Lake Michigan is a testament to that loyalty: Under the same ownership from its construction in 1952 to 2010, the Rambler ranch had undergone multiple additions to meet a growing family's needs. Its new owners also see themselves living in the house for decades to come, so they hired the Egg Design Group to create a clean-lined, flexible space that would support aging in place.

Because setback codes forbid altering the home's footprint, the designers sliced out its center and added a second story. The team showed its commitment to community and the environment by using local craftsmen

and resources—and, alas, Mother Earth responded with weather snafus. A harsh winter filled the site with snow, and custom energy-efficient windows had to be delivered one by one during the spring thaw due to roadway weight limits.

The revamped home enjoys an improved connection with the outdoors: The sunlit, open-plan space suits a range of present and future uses. In the kitchen, custom cabinetry gave every inch a purpose and left room for large prep surfaces and a breakfast banquette. Upstairs common areas will adapt over time, as will the ground-floor master suite. And whenever winter storms arrive, those custom windows will frame serene views of snow falling on treetops while keeping the cold well at bay.

Clockwise from above: Timber detailing begins at the entrance and continues throughout the interior. The multipurpose first-floor den converts into a guest bedroom. Original art and modern furniture lend a lived-in touch. The staircase echoes the entrance's linear detailing. In the upstairs family room, movable LED track lighting washes the beamed ceiling. ➤

3,450 sf
4 bedrooms, 2 ½ bathrooms

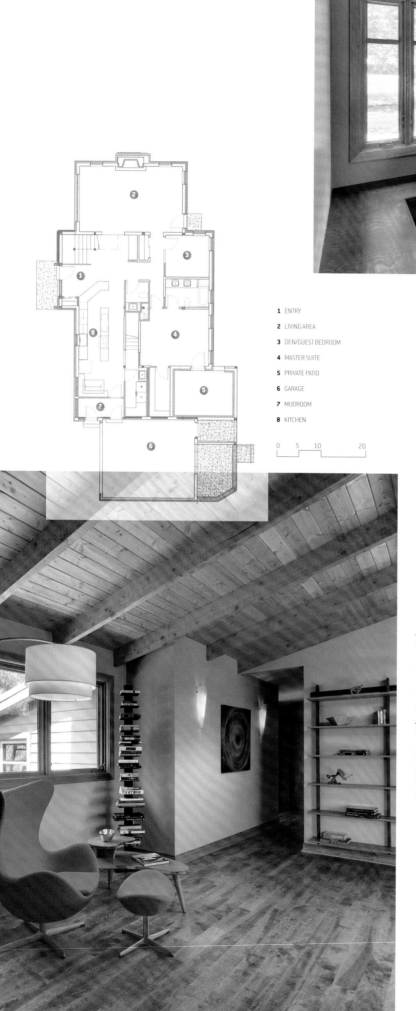

1 ENTRY

2 LIVING AREA

3 DEN/GUEST BEDROOM

4 MASTER SUITE

5 PRIVATE PATIO

6 GARAGE

7 MUDROOM

8 KITCHEN

0   5   10   20

Clockwise from left: Vaulted timber ceilings give the second-floor library the feel of a tree house. The open kitchen incorporates ample storage and a seating banquette to boot. The living room was designed to be easily reconfigured for entertaining; the gas fireplace is remote-controlled. A new mudroom creates space for messy foul-weather gear. The master bath features subway tile with glass tile insets, stainless-steel accents, and radiant subfloor heating. The living room houses a dining area.

PROJECT TEAM LYNN TARRENCE, TODD OVARD, AIA
ARCHITECT OF RECORD 1128 ARCHITECTURAL DESIGN SERVICES
PHOTOGRAPHY TRICIA SHAY

www.theeggdesigngroup.com

city living

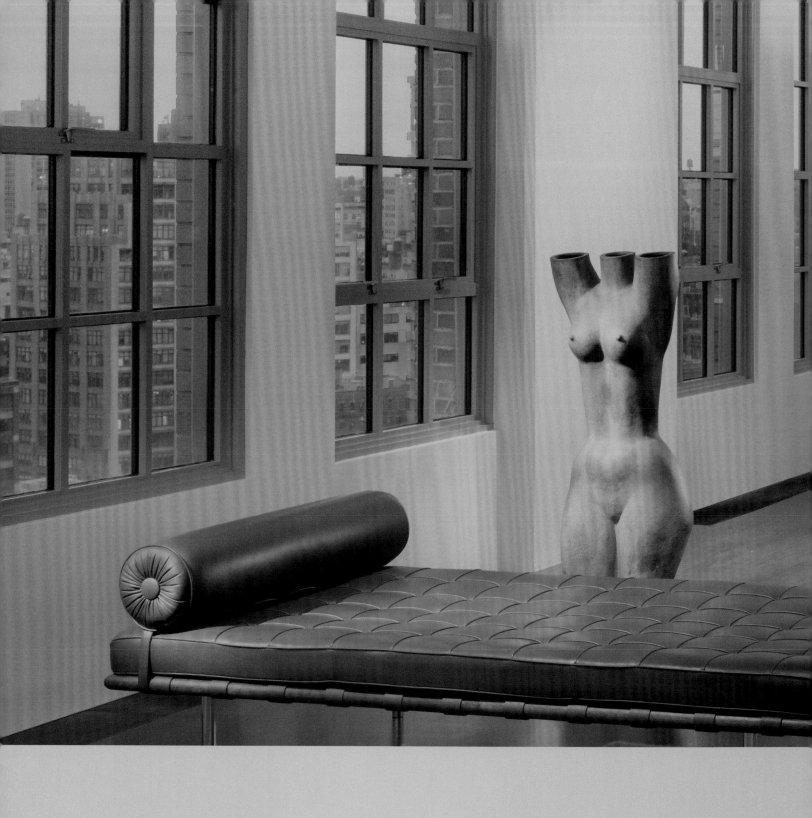

From garden-level apartments and sky-high penthouses to factory conversions and limestone row houses, urban dwellings are truly chameleonic creatures.

Gut renovations, teardowns, new builds, et al mean the face of city living changes as often as the weather. There are some constants, though. Urbanites, invariably a cultured lot, need ample room for their art collections. Square footage comes at a premium so clever space-saving tricks abound—and, of course, abundant glass makes the most of rooftop views and natural illumination. *Let there be light.*

Robert Kaner
Interior Design

UNITED NATIONS PLAZA RESIDENCE, NEW YORK

Clockwise from above: *The balcony levitates 23 stories above Midtown Manhattan. A Todd Hido photograph is mounted on the cerused-oak unit that disguises a structural column; reproduction George Nelson pendants hang from a recycled bamboo–composite canopy. The couple's commitment to artwork achieves fullest expression in the living room, where a photograph by Edward Burtynsky complements a rug commissioned from the painter William Betts.* ➤

The home of fashion and design entrepreneurs Tom Puls and Donna Ricco replays two of Midcentury modernism's greatest hits. Located halfway up a 51-story tower, the co-op enjoys south-facing views of the United Nations complex through full-height windows. And the couple asked interior designer Robert Kaner and architect Rafael Berkowitz to deliver a scheme that nodded to the classic glass-box Case Study Houses.

A core of bathrooms and closets divides the residence—once two apartments—into public and private zones. In the living-area half, unnecessary partitions were removed, giving the circulation a fluid California-mod quality and improving sight lines to the prow-like balcony, which directly gazes on Le Corbusier and Oscar Neimeyer's famed project. One structural column couldn't be removed, so the designers concealed it behind a cerused-oak storage wall. That addition separates a small den from the seamless living/dining area, both of which feature photographs from the couple's avant-garde collection.

Barriers of another sort were struck from the bedrooms. Forgoing distinct sleeping quarters for each of the couple's three sons, the designers devised a communal bunk room with an adjoining shared space for lounge and study. To date, peacekeeping has not been difficult, the clients report; global statesmen a few blocks away should take note.

INTERIOR DESIGN PRINCIPAL ROBERT KANER
ARCHITECT RB ARCHITECT
PHOTOGRAPHY ALBERT VECERKA/ESTO

www.kanerid.com

Clockwise from left:
*Replacing a wall of
closets with a low
built-in credenza
transformed the
master bedroom from
a narrow chamber
with bowling alley—
like proportions into a
gracious haven. The
three boys share a
space for lounging
and studying that
abuts their bedroom,
a configuration akin
to the common rooms
found in dorm suites.
The brothers sleep on
custom beds in the
bunk room. The
cerused-oak partition
provides a break
between the den and
the main living area.
In the dining area,
Eero Saarinen Tulip
chairs surround
a custom resin-top
dining table with a
Herman Miller base.*

1 ENTRY

2 DEN

3 LIVING AREA

4 KITCHEN

5 DINING AREA

6 MASTER SUITE

7 BUNK ROOM

8 KIDS' STUDY/LOUNGE

After the birth of their two children, Tracy and Nick Lehman needed a larger abode but were set on remaining in Manhattan. Serendipitously, they were able to purchase the neighboring unit in their Union Square loft building, allowing them to stay put while doubling their square footage. The couple enlisted copartners Arjun Desai and Katherine Chia to combine the apartments, requesting a seamlessly reconfigured layout that would preserve the easy flow of light and space.

The architects devised a series of flexible, multipurpose living areas that function as backdrops for fine art and a stage for the Lehmans' active lifestyle. Rooms devoted to specific functions—home office, playroom, media room— were designed to connect to or be closed off from adjacent spaces as desired. Such features offer family members maximal visual and social engagement while ensuring that everyone gets some alone time, too.

Partitions and portals in glass or translucent acrylic heighten the sense of airiness and abet the influx of illumination. Bamboo flooring and the liberal use of Corian—in cabinetry, sinks, and even the dining table— reinforce the aura of refinement and expansiveness while artfully withstanding the rigors of family life.

Desai/Chia Architecture

LEHMAN RESIDENCE, NEW YORK

"We devised ways to create a more intimate and engaging environment for the clients' collection of artwork" —ARJUN DESAI AND KATHERINE CHIA

Clockwise from below: Stairs near the kitchen lead to the office. Translucent acrylic custom windows by PK30 System filter light from hallway to office. In the living area, a reconfigurable installation of Algue, by Ronan and Erwan Bouroullec, anchors a pair of Blu Dot sofas and a shag rug from ABC Carpet. The Corian-base kitchen cabinets and island are the architects' design. Glass and crystalline stone tiles combine in the guest bathroom. ➤

From left: *The master bathroom's luminous frosted-glass tiles create a glowing oasis; the Corian sink is a custom Desai/Chia design. Modu-licious #1 nightstands from Blu Dot flank a Ligne Roset Lumeo bed in the master bedroom; the bench is by CB2.*

2,500 sf
3 bedrooms, 3 bathrooms
Expansion/remodel

DESIGN PRINCIPALS ARJUN DESAI, KATHERINE CHIA
PHOTOGRAPHY MARK CRAEMER
www.desaichia.com

1 ENTRY
2 KITCHEN
3 BATHROOM
4 PLAYROOM
5 MASTER SUITE
6 BEDROOM
7 MEDIA ROOM
8 LIVING/DINING AREA
9 OFFICE

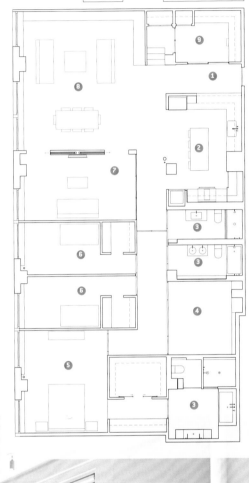

Gary Lee Partners

TRIBECA LOFT, NEW YORK CITY

Clockwise from top: *A Barcelona chaise offers front-row skyline views; in the dining area beyond, a vintage Tommi Parzinger pendant hangs over a bespoke rosewood dining table. The entry's polished-concrete floor segues to polished-walnut planks in the living area, raised two steps to conceal ductwork. BDDW barstools in American black walnut and leather service the square kitchen island.* ➢

Downtown Manhattan lofts are synonymous with creative urban life, and this Tribeca home is no exception. Gary Lee Partners envisioned the tranquil retreat for a pair of art aficionados who craved serenity.

The project marked the first time the building, an industrial factory dating to 1929, would be used for residential purposes. When work began, the space was raw, with exposed mechanicals. To accommodate new ductwork, the designers raised the floor—a move that also greatly improved sight lines. Dozens of new factory-style windows put the emphasis on extensive views of neighboring rooftops and the Hudson River.

The poetic decor embraces the bustling metropolis yet is a world unto itself. Fabric-clad ceiling panels muffle street noise and amplify the Zen-like vibe. Polished-walnut planks unite the vast, open-plan public space; neutral-colored rugs anchoring intimate seating groupings offer the suggestion of distinct rooms. Interior walls are clad in oak paneling, an element Gary Lee deployed to create the appearance of a wooden box inserted into the raw space. Throughout, a controlled spectrum of grays and browns contributes to a feeling of calm—the panoramic view is spectacle enough.

0 20 40 80

1 ENTRY

2 WEST STUDY

3 LIVING AREA

4 DINING AREA

5 MEDIA AREA

6 EAST STUDY/GUEST ROOM

7 MASTER SUITE

8 BATHROOM

9 GYM

10 PANTRY

11 KITCHEN

PROJECT TEAM GARY LEE, ANTHONY LEE, ANDREW GATH, DONNA CORBAT
PHOTOGRAPHY NATHAN KIRKMAN

www.garyleepartners.com

4,000 sf
2 bedrooms,
3 bathrooms

Clockwise from right:
The master bedroom's custom leather headboard and window treatments dampen sound, while a full-height mirror amplifies illumination. One of two studies that abut the main living area; a pocket door slides shut when privacy is needed. Powder room walls are treated to crimson lacquer. During catered events, the kitchen can be kept separate via sliding panel doors. Interior walls throughout are clad in gray-oak millwork.

Delson or Sherman Architects

PARK SLOPE ROW HOUSE, BROOKLYN

Park Slope is renowned for its generous stock of stately limestone row houses. Neighborhood residents are equally well known for their love of all things Midcentury. So when Perla Delson was hired to refresh one of those fabled dwellings for a couple with a young child, she knew just what to do: integrate traditional and modern elements in a family-friendly—and borough-appropriate—way.

Historic details were meticulously restored, then juxtaposed with modernist insertions: Sleek cast-glass globe lights were selected to play off the ornate wood staircase, for example. Original stained-glass windows lent inspiration for the doorway leading from dining room to deck; it now sports stripes of textured glass.

Open-air rooms in the backyard and the roof deck got classic bluestone flooring, while panels of cast iron and glass pave the new rear terrace.

Infrastructure was also brought up to date. Among the sustainable improvements are a whole-house fan, a high-efficiency boiler, and an insulated building envelope and windows. Targeted radiant-heat floors are covered in quarter-sawn solid-white oak or softer touches like rugs in custom angora shag and wild silk.

The old-meets-new theme extends to the home's furnishings, too. Kiki Dennis Interiors assembled an amicable mix of vintage items that perfectly complement Delson or Sherman's elegant design—and are all perfectly Brooklyn-worthy.

4,700 sf
4 bedrooms, 3 bathrooms

PROJECT TEAM PERLA DELSON, JEFF SHERMAN, JOHN MEALY
FURNISHINGS KIKI DENNIS INTERIORS
GENERAL CONTRACTOR TATRA RENOVATION
PHOTOGRAPHY JASON SCHMIDT
www.delsonsherman.com

Clockwise from opposite: A sleek boomerang-shape sectional by Planum Furniture and a Century Furniture coffee table define the living room's seating area; the flooring is low-maintenance faux wood porcelain. A trio of cloisonnés takes pride of place on the coffee table. The dining area is adjacent to the kitchen, making entertaining a breeze. ➤

Business and pleasure can indeed mix when a designer devises an open floor plan for her own home—which happens to double as her office. A year after purchasing a unit in Arris Loft, a former factory building in Long Island City, Trini Lam embarked on a redesign. She and her husband wanted a space where they could cook and entertain their brood of married children and grandchildren. Lam found the original layout confining and featureless and wanted to accentuate the high ceilings, tall windows, and unusual architectural elements.

Lam opened up the great room by removing the wall separating it from her home office and reconfiguring the master suite. She now has space for a two-part dining table that seats 16, as well as an intimate entertaining area with a 15-foot-long bar-height countertop along the window. Floating above the living area, a piano-shape drop ceiling plays off the curve of a newly exposed support column. A variety of lighting fixtures—from pendant and chandelier to dimmable fluorescent and modular downlight—allow her to customize the mood.

The family now has plenty of room to interact in when they gather together. And Lam's visiting clients can see exactly how she applied her design skills to envision a spacious home that's warm, inviting, and party-ready.

Trini Design

LONG ISLAND CITY LOFT, NEW YORK

1,900 sf
2 bedrooms,
2 ½ bathrooms

Clockwise from left:
The newly opened-up
entertaining space
features custom
10-foot French doors,
a Caesarstone-top
kitchen island by
Jonathan Arnold,
and a bar-height
counter along the
window wall. A pair
of Calligaris dining
tables seat 16;
underlighting below
the rear counter
creates a soft glow.
The Vitra dining chairs
are by Maarten Van
Severen. Above the
living area, a 19-by-
10-foot drop ceiling
plays off the curves of
the existing structural
column. Dimmable
fluorescents in the
bedroom and an
inviting Century
Furniture bed impart
a mellow vibe.

DESIGN PRINCIPAL TRINI LAM
PHOTOGRAPHY TOM SIBLEY

www.trinidesign.com

EliasElias AR

WEST 12TH STREET CONDOMINIUM
NEW YORK

The architecture and interior design firm, with offices in Miami and Guadalajara, was contracted to turn a three-bedroom waterfront apartment into a more spacious two-bedroom. In the process, the team carved out two full baths and dressing rooms, a powder room, an eat-in kitchen, a combination living/dining area, and a media area. The apartment is perched on the southwest corner of the building, a luxury condo tower overlooking the Hudson.

With views this stunning, who needs art? The collection scattered throughout makes a compelling argument. Curated with a consultant, the paintings, photographs,

and sculptures exert a quiet though powerful presence. Fiery accents of red and orange spark against the soothing earth-tone palette and exotic woods.

The lush terrace, which measures upwards of 1,500 square feet, is open on three sides to take maximum advantage of the riverside location; it also can be accessed from any of three rooms. Diverse greenery thrives in the custom wood planters bordering the space, and a complete irrigation system ensures it will stay that way.

The space is spare, open, and bright: Inside or outside, from any vantage point, the views please and dazzle.

Clockwise from top:
An abstract sculpture in the Paul Evans vein—which later reveals itself as figural—presides over the living/dining area. A custom Odabashian International rug helps delineate the light-filled dining space. The intimate eat-in kitchen. ➤

1,500 sf terrace
Conversion from 3 bedrooms to 2

PROJECT TEAM ALEXIS ELIAS (LEAD DESIGNER), RICHARD ELIAS,
MAYRA LÓPEZ, DAVID COHEN, GISELA ANDERSON
ARCHITECT OF RECORD VICTORIA BENATAR
PHOTOGRAPHY ANTOINE BOOTZ
www.eliaselias.net

Clockwise from right:
The bedroom of the
master suite. Many
furnishings—this
dining room table,
chairs, and chandelier
among them—are the
handiwork of Hudson
Furniture. City
Beautiful Carpentry
custom built the
terrace deck and
planters; the Organic
Gardener landscaped.
A double-wide portal
bisects the living and
dining areas.

MR Architecture + Decor

TRIBECA PENTHOUSE, NEW YORK

Clockwise from right:
In the living room, an Eero Aarnio Ball chair joins a mobile flatscreen and minimalist hearth. The office is furnished with a 1960s Bodil Kjaer rosewood pedestal desk, custom mohair shag rug, and a Jeffrey Milstein photograph. Near the bedrooms, stainless-steel modular shelving converts a corridor into auxiliary work space. The custom stainless-steel kitchen opens to a spacious dining room with Eero Saarinen Tulip chairs and a David Weeks chandelier. In the master suite, a stainless-steel bed is suspended beside a glassed-in bathroom; the steel staircase leads to the roof deck.

Sometimes a space needs a makeover; sometimes it needs a make*under*. The client, a private investor, had already completed a cosmetic revamp of his airy penthouse. But it just wasn't *him*. So he hired MR Architecture + Decor to envision a better use of space, a more refined design palette, more light, and a more elegantly manly vibe.

A near-total gut renovation followed, leaving untouched only the masonry perimeter, original fenestration, brick arch vaults, and structural columns. Tearing down interior partitions helped establish sight lines to all three window walls, including one spanning the entire 70-foot length of the living area—now connected to the dining and kitchen spaces. The private quarters, formerly a two-bedroom/two-bath wing, were expanded into a four-bedroom/four-bath layout that's ideal for hosting guests and entertaining.

Clean-lined industrial finishes honored the building's heritage while lending masculine cool. Apart from a marine-grade plywood walk-in closet, custom cabinetry is stainless steel throughout; so are sliding doors, in a thumbs-up to the existing fire portals. MR painted the brick perimeter walls and vaulted ceilings a timeless flat white to maximize the new abundance of natural light.

The loft's crowning triumph is the master suite, with transparent glass walls between bed and bath that allow a pair of skylights to illuminate every inch of the space. Even the bed and stair hang from the ceiling, as if to embody the delicate balance achieved.

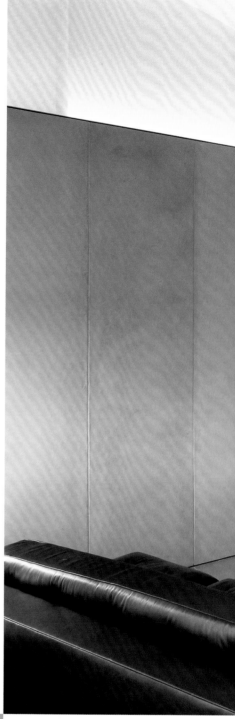

4,000 sf
4 bedrooms, 4 bathrooms

DESIGN PRINCIPAL DAVID MANN
PHOTOGRAPHY ERIC LAIGNEL
www.mrarch.com

bStudio

GRAMERCY PARK GARDEN APARTMENT, NEW YORK

Clockwise from above: *The living room, which faces the patio and garden, is festooned with a complementary mix of fabric patterns. One of the client's chic handbag designs, displayed like fine art against a wall papered in a lattice print. Chinese Chippendale–style seats repeat the lattice motif, while upholstered chairs provide a plusher perch at the dining table's ends. Even the books are artfully arranged, stacked to form impromptu pedestals for objets. Natural materials like stone, hemp, and wicker temper the living room's bold graphics.* ➤

A residence in a historic 19th-century former boarding school teaches a stylish lesson in sustainable design. Paints are low-VOC, bulbs are metal halide, wall coverings are hemp, the nursery's rift-sawn oak floor planks were salvaged from an old barn, triple-pane windows and doors are airtight, patio slate was sourced locally, and the efficient HVAC system is controlled by timed, zoned thermostats. Even brick removed during interior demolition was used to build a rear extension and garden wall.

The latter move helped achieve the main goals of this renovation: to bring in more light (without altering the landmarked limestone facade) and to provide garden views from rear-facing rooms. Newly brightened, the tailored interior is a quiet riot of color and pattern—appropriate, since the client is a handbag designer. Removing walls and annexing alcoves served to double size of the kitchen, converting it to an open-plan space that lets the client mingle with guests while cooking at her robin's-egg blue range. In the hushed living area, with its navy and cream palette, graphic florals mix with pert geometrics. Spirited throw pillows accessorize the space—as do a few artfully displayed handbags in vibrant hues.

CHANEL

Slim Aarons · A Place in the Sun

Blahník by Boman Shoes, Photographs, Conversation

Mother

DESIGN PRINCIPAL BREANNA CARLSON
ARCHITECT OF RECORD BRIAN GILLEN
GENERAL CONTRACTOR NTS CONTRACTING
PHOTOGRAPHY BREANNA CARLSON/BSTUDIO (1, 6, 8, 10),
RACHEL McGINN (2–5, 7, 9, 11)
www.bstudio-ad.com

Clockwise from left: The designer reused existing crystal fixtures, such as this pendant in a master suite closet. Ceramic subway tile segues to stainless steel above the range. The master bedroom's slim canopy frame ensures the snug confines feel airy; floral drapes and a foliage-themed pendant invite the outdoors in. Triple-pane windows update the landmarked facade of the garden-level apartment, formed by combining a studio and one-bedroom. Hand-painted 19th-century wallpaper discovered in a closet was preserved behind acrylic. Hemp wall covering adds texture.

1 ENTRY
2 BATHROOM
3 NURSERY
4 PATIO
5 LIVING AREA
6 DINING AREA
7 KITCHEN
8 MASTER BEDROOM

0   5   10   20

Sand Studios

MEHTA RESIDENCE, MIAMI BEACH

The San Francisco–based firm describes itself as balancing "minimal aesthetics" with "material expression." That explains the restrained luxuriousness that distinguishes this apartment overlooking the ocean; carefully selected finishes speak for themselves through color and texture.

Indian rosewood is the veneer of choice, its richly figured grain dressing up walls and furniture alike. Marble—polished, honed, variegated—predominates as well. The kitchen and master bedroom feature a fine white stone with gold veining, an aqueous blue version adorns the walls of a guest bath, and an unusual orange variety lines the powder room's walls. Complementing the marble are other quietly impactful surfaces: brushed limestone flooring, river stone accents, stainless-steel frames, exposed concrete shear walls.

Lighting is simultaneously unobtrusive and dramatic, with many sculptural custom fixtures. Indirect illumination softly accentuates the textures of materials, showcasing their imperfect organic beauty like works of art.

Finally, there's liberal use of glass, which acts as walls in spots, forms sliding panels, and composes the coffee table. The glazing also offers up a metaphor for the project's overarching concept: Principal Larissa Sand aimed for a sense of openness, transparency, and connectedness that would reflect the landscape outside. Thus the residence should—and does—project an unadorned and soothing cool, with far-reaching sight lines and understated natural tones. It's easy to make yourself at home.

Clockwise from top:
A glass wall—fitted with an opaque motor- ized shade—is all that separates living and sleeping quarters. Full-height glazing between the guest room's bathing and sleeping quarters puts the blue marble wet zone on display. The powder room features walls of vivid paprika-hued marble. Custom built-ins make for a hyperfunctional master bedroom. The entry hallway, accented with black marble, doubles as an art gallery; the light fixture is crafted from etched science glass. In the living room, a sliding glass-and- steel panel exposes a rosewood-lined office.

3,000 sf
2 bedrooms, 3 bathrooms

DESIGN PRINCIPAL LARISSA SAND
PHOTOGRAPHY KEN HAYDEN
www.sandstudios.com

Gary Lee Partners

GOLD COAST CONDOMINIUM, CHICAGO

Clockwise from above: *Custom cabinetry envelops the study, furnished with a Christian Liaigre daybed. The living room sofa, by Chai Ming Studios, is accented with custom pillows. In the entry, artworks by James Brooks and David Bierk meet a Barovier & Toso glass chandelier and a walnut table, also by Chai Ming Studios.* ➤

The Windy City's Gold Coast is aptly named: It's all about luxury and affluence, from the tony shopping destinations to the posh lakeside apartment buildings. This condo by Gary Lee Partners fits right in with its stately neighbors. But while sophistication was paramount to the clients, so was comfort: The couple desired an easygoing space for relaxing and hosting guests. Existing partitions were thus demolished to combine the living room, dining room, and study into a fluid sweep of space, one that encourages entertaining and highlights spectacular Lake Michigan vistas.

Customized elements lend a tailored touch throughout, from silk accent pillows and pinch-pleat draperies to the living room's distinctive bronze fireplace surround, a minimalist sculpture in its own right. The kitchen, outfitted with marble countertops, sleek appliances, and bespoke cabinetry, can be concealed from the adjacent entry and dining room via sliding pocket doors. Next to the elegant yet cozy study is the master suite, encompassing an understated sleeping chamber, an opulent bathroom, and a spacious walk-in closet. The well-appointed guest quarters were sited on the apartment's opposite end to give overnighters privacy—and their own waterfront view.

1 ENTRY

2 POWDER ROOM

3 KITCHEN

4 GUEST SUITE

5 DINING AREA

6 LIVING AREA

7 STUDY

8 MASTER BEDROOM

9 MASTER BATHROOM

10 LAUNDRY ROOM

0   10   20   40

3,500 sf
2 bedrooms,
2½ bathrooms

PROJECT TEAM GARY LEE, BETH EVELAND
PHOTOGRAPHY NATHAN KIRKMAN

www.garyleepartners.com

Clockwise from right:
A light neutral palette establishes a sense of calm in the master bedroom, where a Giacommeti bench by Porta Romana anchors a custom bed by Chai Ming Studios. The dining room's silk area rug is by Tai Ping Carpets. Bella glass pendants by Niche Modern command attention in the kitchen. Cabinetry above the living room's custom bronze fireplace surround conceals a television. The powder room features Laura Kirar's Vir Stil bronze basin set and handpainted wallpaper by Studio E. In the master bath, slabs of Calacatta marble are set aglow by a pair of custom crystal chandeliers.

A minimalist apartment in a new Miami Beach high-rise reaches maximum style potential when things are kept simple. The key was getting to work before the building was complete—indeed, before the concrete was even poured. Principal Larissa Sand upgraded the standard unit template to an open layout, where sparely detailed materials such as marble, wood, mirror, Corian, and steel form a fluid backdrop for the client's collection of contemporary art.

The tall panels of the kitchen's Italian cabinetry system mimic—and thus blend in with—the walnut millwork used elsewhere; flush handles are a near-invisible interruption to the clean-lined design. Concealed or subdued utilities are recurring themes, with the intent, explains Sand, not to underscore function but to "draw one in to a more emotional experience of the environment." In another instance, a vanity in the master bathroom is constructed from the same painterly gray-and-white marble used for the walls, floor, and sunken soaking tub; the whole room appears carved from a single block of stone. Throughout the loftlike space, continuous use of material and cantilevered elements conspire to create a floating feel—a device that artfully bridges indoors and out.

Sand Studios

GUTTMAN RESIDENCE, MIAMI BEACH

3 bedrooms,
4 bathrooms

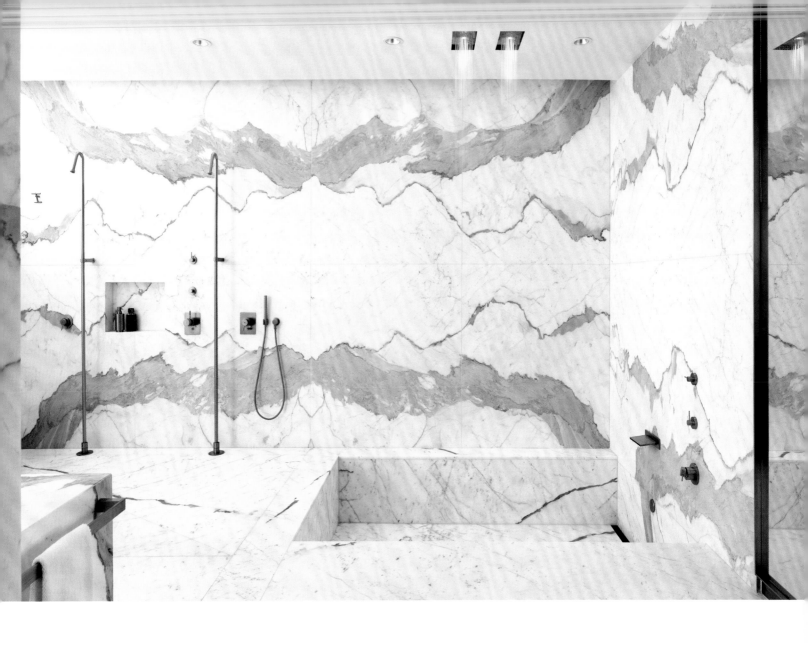

PROJECT TEAM LARISSA SAND, ZACHARY MADDRY, BENJAMIN DAMRON, ALAN DOUGHERTY
PHOTOGRAPHY KEN HAYDEN
www.sandstudios.com

Clockwise from opposite top: In the master bathroom, a backlit custom mirror and a cantilevered counter conjure a feeling of weightlessness. The room's marble-clad wet area features a double shower and sunken soaking tub. Graceful proportions in the guest room don't compete with the views beyond the sheer draperies. Subtle veining unites wood and stone in the powder room. A reflective range hood in the kitchen hides in plain sight. A mirrored, slatted partition separates the sculpture-filled entry from the living area.

modern family

Does the phrase "family home" conjure a classic nuclear unit living under one staid suburban roof? Think again.

Some of these dwellings were designed to house expectant parents, spirited twin boys, or empty nesters (or about-to-bes); others were for blended or multigenerational families. But all demanded creative solutions. Out-of-the-box thinking sparked savvy spaces such as a multilevel Monte Carlo apartment that features a floor per generation, Manhattan lofts that pair sturdy furnishings with blue-chip art, and abodes that offer kids and adults separate sanctums—alongside zones for clan-wide get-togethers or jam sessions. *Talk about family values.*

Betty Wasserman Art & Interiors

MACDOUGAL STREET LOFT
NEW YORK

A family home has to withstand family demands. So when a couple with twin boys contacted Betty Wasserman to design their floor-through apartment in an 1891 industrial building, the brief was to create an abode able to take all the abuse two kids and a dog could offer, without losing the modern elegance the parents desired.

Wasserman divided the West Village loft into a four-bedroom/five-bath layout that included the all-important playroom. There, a clever dual-purpose crimson sectional with ottomans converts to a queen-size bed for overnight guests. She installed custom storage everywhere she could

and utilized her 20-year experience as a curator to fill the walls with blue-chip art and commissioned works.

Furniture designer André Joyau crafted numerous bespoke pieces, including a showstopper of a dining room table: Twelve feet long and made of walnut, it's positioned so diners can contemplate the Empire State Building. Other furnishings were custom made from salvaged beams, such as the raft-style cocktail table in the living room and the screen dividing the dining area and media room.

With appointments both functional and fashionable, Wasserman clearly designed a home to live—and play—in.

Clockwise from above: Wasserman's daughter, Milly, races down the art-filled hallway gallery, cushioned by a Stephanie Odegard custom felt runner. A painting by Margaret Evangeline hangs in the foyer. The playroom's Dennis Miller Associates armchair is covered in Pierre Frey fabric. A custom end-grain beech divider separates the dining/living area and media room. ➤

Clockwise from left:
A Joel Perlman bronze accents the raft-style coffee table; on the back wall is a commissioned "text portrait" painting by Gary Gissler incorporating hundreds of words—some viewable only via magnifying glass—that hold special meaning to the family. A Hilton Brothers photograph hangs in the gallery hallway. André Joyau fabricated the living room's sculptural blackened-steel fireplace surround. The same material traces the living/dining room's archways and forms an armature for the end-grain screen. ➤

"Choosing multitasking furnishings, assigning each area a practical purpose, and adding storage maximized the space"—BETTY WASSERMAN

Clockwise from left:
In the playroom, a pair of framed abstract works by Margaret Evangeline pick up the red tones of the Pierre Frey drapery fabric and the custom sectional/guest bed; the pendant is by David Trubridge. Louise Crandell was commissioned to hand paint a mural in the boys' bedroom. A luminous cluster of glass Bocci pendants spotlights the dining table's stack of Rina Menardi ceramics.

1 FOYER
2 MEDIA ROOM
3 LIVING/DINING AREA
4 KITCHEN
5 BEDROOM
6 MASTER BATHROOM
7 MASTER BEDROOM
8 PLAYROOM
9 LAUNDRY ROOM

DESIGN PRINCIPAL BETTY WASSERMAN
PHOTOGRAPHY ERIC LAIGNEL
www.bettywasserman.com

Clockwise from opposite top: The master bathroom features a Wetstyle soaking tub and a custom teak shower floor. The walk-in shower isn't for the parents' enjoyment only: they jokingly refer to it as the boys' water park. Heptagon Creations fabricated the master suite's custom bed, which separates sleeping and dressing areas; the daybed is by Chris Lehrecke and the single-piece wood fan by Boffi. Limed-oak planks from Stone Source lend a textured yet tailored touch to the master bath's custom double vanity. Circular elements help soften the foyer's boxy proportions: a BDDW mirror, Stephanie Odegard shag rug, and a DAB glass-bulb chandelier.

4,600 sf
4 bedrooms, 5 bathrooms

W24 LOFT, NEW YORK

In troubleshooting a previously dark, cavernous Chelsea loft, Desai/Chia's best thinking was done inside the box—well, make that two. Rather than rely on solid walls to divvy the open plan, Arjun Desai and Katherine Chia separated living and sleeping quarters via a pair of wood-and-glass boxes housing bathrooms and storage. Arrayed in an L, the pods are capped by continuous clerestories that transmit light in both directions, coaxing sunshine into the interior spaces while brightening the loft proper with a lanternlike glow.

A play of privacy and permeability distinguishes other enclosures, too. An airy study, with stunning views through the street-facing window wall, is veiled in acid-etched glass shingles, softly diffusing daylight. The same treatment clads the master bathroom for a similar lit-from-within effect.

Clever adjacencies further order the layout. Spanning the pod that anchors the kitchen is a 24-foot-long stainless-steel prep/dining counter with translucent sliding doors. Sleeping spaces are grouped at the loft's rear, where the children's bedroom, playroom, and bathroom form a separate suite. This self-contained zone accommodates the boisterousness of play dates and hide-and-seek—a game the loft's evanescent walls would seem to win.

Clockwise from top:
The glass clerestory above the kitchen cabinets funnels light into the powder room/ storage pod behind; Cappellini chairs surround a dining table by Matthew Hilton. Acid-etched glass shingles clad the master bathroom, while the pod beyond is sheathed in solid-stock wood slats. The children's play-room connects to their bathroom, at left. A view from the study to the master bath, both enclosed in acid-etched glass. ➤

Desai/Chia Architecture

4,000 sf
2 bedrooms, 3 bathrooms

A sinuous UNStudio sofa snakes through the living area alongside Verner Panton side chairs and an aluminum Giovannitti table; the central kitchen was designed to be the focus of the loft. ⬎

"The boxes act as beacons, providing illumination from above; they activate the ceiling plane and enhance the flow of light in an otherwise dark interior" —KATHERINE CHIA AND ARJUN DESAI

1 ENTRY

2 POWDER ROOM

3 STUDY

4 LIVING/DINING/MEDIA AREA

5 KITCHEN

6 PLAYROOM

7 KIDS' BEDROOM

8 MASTER SUITE

0   5   10   20

Clockwise from opposite: The glass-shingle partition draws light into the master bathroom, fitted with a freestanding tub. Nobi sconces illuminate a Wetstyle sink in the children's ceramic-tiled bathroom. The continuous glass clerestory capping the kitchen pod serves to dematerialize the structure; floors are sealed concrete.

PROJECT TEAM KATHERINE CHIA, ARJUN DESAI
CONTRACTOR GIOVANNITTI
LIGHTING CONSULTANT CHRISTINE SCIULLI LIGHT + DESIGN
MECHANICAL ENGINEER SIMON RODKIN CONSULTING ENGINEERS
STRUCTURAL ENGINEER MURRAY ENGINEERING
PHOTOGRAPHY PAUL WARCHOL

www.desaichia.com

Federico Delrosso Architects

When Federico Delrosso was approached to design a home in the heart of Monte Carlo, the clients' blended family occasioned a blended residence: three existing apartments—one with a mezzanine—fused into a single 2,282-square-foot space.

The Milanese architect unified the four floors by constructing an internal staircase, separate from the building's stairs. Like branches of a family tree, each level became home to a different generation. The lowest floor is devoted to a trio of sleeping quarters for the older, more independent children; the parents and youngest child occupy the intimate and compact second floor; and the loftlike top space contains a double-height living area and kitchen for entertaining extended family and friends. "The

house is a kind of exoskeleton in which human relations develop and find their balance," notes Delrosso.

To further strengthen the ties between levels, the architect visualized a vertical line running through each floor, manifested in an elegant steel cable that attaches to the skylight's central girder. He also chose a single wood, zebrano, for all the doors, partitions, and custom furniture by Habitat MC. Its natural, almost wild texture lends warmth to the palette of gray-stained oak flooring and white-painted walls. "The zebrano is a neutral element that supports the future evolution of the decor—it's almost a metaphor for family relationships," Delrosso concludes.

1 ENTRY

2 LIVING AREA

3 DINING AREA

4 KITCHEN

5 STAIRCASE

6 POWDER ROOM

PRINCIPAL FEDERICO DELROSSO
CUSTOM FURNISHINGS HABITAT MC
PHOTOGRAPHY FAUSTO MAZZA

www.federicodelrosso.com

Clockwise from opposite: *Zebrano furnishings and partitions perk up the living room; flooring throughout is gray-stained oak. Partially screened by a zebrano partition, a new staircase connects the four levels. The master bathroom features a glass-wall shower. A skylight illuminates the stairwell. The mezzanine lounge and study; visible to the right is the symbolic cable, Delrosso's metaphor for strength and lightness.*

2,282 sf
5 bedrooms, 5 bathrooms

WATTS STREET LOFT, NEW YORK

Studio Tractor Architecture

Pale blues and amber-toned wood form the delicately sophisticated color palette of this Tribeca apartment. The clients had lived in the neighborhood for several years prior to having children and wanted to stay there as their family grew. So they purchased a raw loft and challenged principals Mark Kolodziejczak and Michael Tower with transforming the open-plan space into a nuclear two-bedroom/two-bath layout—while maintaining the expansiveness of the original configuration.

To maximize daylight, the living/dining area and kitchen face a wall of tall windows, and the bedrooms have etched-glass doors with transoms that allow sunlight to pass through. Tower explains that the design approach was guided by circulation: how one enters and moves through the space. "Moments are either framed or expressed," he explains. For example, a foyer was established by "thickening" the walls on either side with deep closets, thereby bracketing the entry. The closets are clad in teak veneer, the same woodwork used for the kitchen cabinetry and the living room built-ins, establishing cohesion. Cool touches—rich statuary marble, crisp grays, textiles in subtle oceanic hues—play off the warm wood finishes. Who wouldn't want to grow up in such a space?

Clockwise from top:
Throughout the open-plan loft, Studio Tractor created frisson between cool-toned fabrics and warm teak finishes. The living room reflects Studio Tractor's design philosophy: simplicity of expression via rich materials, crisp geometries, and careful modulation of light. Etched glass funnels illumination into the master bedroom; the passageway to the en suite bathroom is lined with closets. ➤

1,500 sf
2 bedrooms, 2 bathrooms

PROJECT TEAM DESIGN PRINCIPALS: MARK KOLODZIEJCZAK, MICHAEL TOWER,
DESIGN STAFF: ANDREW BARWICK
PHOTOGRAPHY CHUCK CHOI

www.studiotractor.com

From top: Entry closets, living room built-ins, and the custom Henrybuilt kitchen are teak veneer with a natural finish. In the master bathroom, white tiles, an oversize mirror, and a glass shower divider keep the look airy and spacious.

1 ENTRY

2 STORAGE CLOSET

3 KITCHEN

4 DINING AREA

5 LIVING AREA

6 BEDROOM

7 MASTER BEDROOM

8 MASTER BATHROOM

9 BATHROOM

0   10   20   40

Clockwise from top: *The polished travertine topping a pair of Lucite coffee tables provides plenty of surface area while heightening the living room's light, open feel. The ground-floor entry is clad in leather panels with chrome details and features a custom mirror. Chairs upholstered in electric blue lend a playful edge to the formal dining area, furnished with a Macassar dining table; the black glass chandelier is custom made.* ➤

Divided into four apartments by a previous owner, this classic brownstone was poised to house a single family once again. Warren Bohn and Kelly Woodruff were contracted to transform it into a lively, modern setting befitting an active young brood.

With four children, a large extended family, and a wide social circle, the homeowners planned to entertain regularly. They requested not only separate kid-friendly and adult-only areas but also both formal and informal spaces to accommodate groups of varying sizes.

The casual entertainment quarters are now sensibly sited on the ground floor, which includes a leather-paneled entrance hall, a den conducive to gatherings, and a sizable playroom with backyard access. The next level houses a more "grown-up" zone. A foyer with powder room separates the ethereally appointed living room—with walk-in bar—from the large dining room, warmed by a three-sided fireplace in Macassar ebony and marble. The custom kitchen, designed in white Anigre with stainless-steel frames and backsplash tiles, completes the floor.

Children's bedrooms and baths occupy two levels, along with a family room and terrace; also here is the private adult lounge, a haven for working or unwinding complete with computer station, walk-in kitchenette, and minibar. The entire top floor is devoted to the master suite, which houses an exquisite marble bathroom.

The home once divided is now happily reunited.

Bohn Associates

UPPER EAST SIDE BROWNSTONE, NEW YORK

1 FRONT YARD

2 ENTRY

3 FOYER

4 POWDER ROOM

5 DEN

6 PLAYROOM

7 LAUNDRY ROOM

8 BACKYARD

0   5   10   20

8,000 sf
6 bedrooms, 8 bathrooms

Clockwise from above: The centerpiece of the master bedroom is the outsize bed, with a headboard framed in silver leaf and upholstered in the same fabric as the settee at its foot. Turquoise tiles flank the mirror in a boy's bathroom. Sleek gray-stained wood cabinetry trimmed in white lacquer lines the walk-through dressing room. A bold glass mosaic enlivens the formal powder room. White dominates the adult lounge. Striated Linac marble and glass tiles backed with silver leaf animate the spa-like master bath.

PROJECT TEAM WARREN BOHN, KELLY WOODRUFF, SILVIA CARLUCCI
PHOTOGRAPHY PAMELA MASTERS

www.bohndesign.com

5,500 sf
4 bedrooms, 3 bathrooms,
2 half bathrooms

Clockwise from below: In the kitchen, casual meals take place from the comfort of Harry Bertoia barstools. The dining table and chairs are by Chai Ming Studios; antique French sconces, refurbished by New Metal Crafts, flank a pair of Robert Longo lithographs. Chai Ming also designed the living room's custom sofa, side tables, and chairs; the rug is by Tai Ping Carpets and the photograph, Michael Eastman. ➤

NORTH SHORE RESIDENCE
HIGHLAND PARK, ILLINOIS

Gary Lee Partners

After spending decades in the same house, a 1950s modernist-inspired dwelling, the owners decided it was high time to undertake a renovation and addition. The couple tapped Gary Lee Partners to reconfigure the interior into a roomier-feeling space: one that would be more hospitable to family gatherings with adult children and grandchildren.

The design team devised a seamless, open-plan space with a combined living/dining room at its heart. To one side of this family lounging hub is the expanded master suite and the wife's office; opposite is the den, kitchen, informal dining area, playroom, and—adjoining the latter—the husband's den. The placement of the his-and-hers sanctums allows the grandparents to keep an eye on the kids while maintaining a slight buffer from the action.

Accommodating the couple's large art collection was also a priority, not to mention a challenge. The clients wanted the flexibility to rotate pieces without disturbing the "finished" look of the space and requested that the decor not veer too gallerylike or sterile. Those aims were achieved via appropriately scaled walls, furniture and rugs chosen to lend softness, and a nature-inspired palette. Hues were drawn from the the browns and greens of the surrounding trees, the moody gray Chicago sky, and the crisp blues of the backyard pool—now more visible through newly enlarged windows.

PROJECT TEAM GARY LEE, SUSAN EICHINGER
ARCHITECT OF RECORD COHEN+HACKER ARCHITECTS
BUILDER SCOTT SIMPSON BUILDERS
PHOTOGRAPHY TONY SOLURI
www.garyleepartners.com

Clockwise from near left: *The playroom is furnished with Morlen Sinoway chairs and a Chai Ming Studios sofa. In the master suite, a pair of Holly Hunt benches anchor a bed and nightstands, also Chai Ming creations. Crystal sconces in the master bathroom make sparkling use of streaming sunlight. A constellation of Bocci pendants are clustered above the eat-in kitchen's dining area. In the wife's office, which also acts as a sitting room, a custom Chai Ming desk and credenza join DBC Deco club chairs and a settee by Benjamin Storck; the original windows were replaced with larger panes to better embrace the view.*

1 ENTRY

2 MASTER BEDROOM

3 MASTER BATHROOM

4 WALK-IN CLOSET/DRESSING ROOM

5 WIFE'S DEN

6 FAMILY ROOM

7 HUSBAND'S DEN

8 PLAYROOM

9 KITCHEN

0   10   20   40

Jaque Bethke for Pure Design Environments

FOR ART'S SAKE, MINNESOTA RIVER VALLEY

New real-estate listings come to life at the Parade of Homes, a semiannual event held in the Twin Cities area, when the doors of speculative and model houses are opened to aspiring nesters. It was there that a pair of newlyweds fell hard for a residence with interiors by Minneapolis-based designer Jaque Bethke. But alas, the couple didn't have subdivisions in mind: The Twin Cities natives wanted a new abode that would combine the best qualities of their two current addresses—a Chicago condo and a Minnesota residence—into a single dream home where they could raise a family. So they hired both developer and designer to re-create the domestic scene in a far more secluded location: on a bluff overlooking the Minnesota River Valley.

To capitalize on the views, Bethke adapted the plan of the Parade of Homes model. Another departure was the 1,000-gallon tropical aquarium, which Bethke used to divide the kitchen and hearth room from the more formal public areas. (Her first foray into giant-fish-tank territory was with the Rainforest Cafe, which was conceived some 20 years ago.) A neutral color palette and textured finishes ensure that the homeowners and guests alike focus on the natural bounty—both outdoors and in.

10,000 sf
5 bedrooms,
7 bathrooms

Clockwise from top:
The downstairs theater is lit with color-changing LEDs. The lower level was designed as a hub for entertaining friends and family, complete with a full-size bar and glass-enclosed, temperature-controlled wine storage. The living room floor is finished in 3-by-6-foot granite slabs that complement the tones in the barrel-vaulted ceiling. ➤

Clockwise from above: *Beyond the loungelike hearth room, the kitchen island's dye-infused glass countertop resonates with the nearby aquarium—and provides a vivid contrast to cabinets and millwork veneered in bird's-eye maple. In the home spa, LED strips were placed to highlight veining within the onyx surfaces. The lower level also features an extensive home gym and a sauna. The large and airy master bedroom incorporates a generous seating area. The tropical fish tank measures 48 feet square.*

1 GARAGE

2 ENTRY

3 STUDY

4 GREAT ROOM

5 DINING AREA

6 KITCHEN

7 DINETTE/OFFICE

8 DECK

9 MASTER BEDROOM

10 MASTER BATHROOM

0   10   20   40

DESIGN PRINCIPAL JAQUE BETHKE
PHOTOGRAPHY TODD BUCHANAN

www.jaquebethke.com

Charles J. Nafie Architects

CLASSIC PARK AVENUE APARTMENT, NEW YORK

The classic eight is the holy grail of New York City real estate; the phrase alone brings to mind images of Belle Époque grandeur and comfort. Renovating one such treasure on Park Avenue, Charles Nafie took a more nuanced—and slightly contrarian—view of that standard. Carved into a series of formal rooms that demanded children's best behavior and presumed help from staff, the domicile exuded the pomp of a period drama. But the circumstances weren't conducive to the very modern lives of a husband and wife and their two kids.

The remodel pays respect to the apartment's historic vernacular while embodying contemporary principles about family dynamics. Using the original foyer as a hinge, Nafie located the main living areas at opposite corners of the floor plan. Casual pastimes rule the larger of the two spaces, a combination dining/family/media room that's adjacent to the kitchen. (Bridging antique and modern, the large flatscreen TV is framed within traditionally styled mahogany cabinetry.) More buttoned-up activities occur in the living room, where deeply coffered ceilings enhance the generous prewar proportions—and where the kids go to engage in analogue-era piano practice.

Clockwise from above: The kitchen, brightened by an antiqued-glass backsplash, opens to a family room devoted to dining and leisure activities. A coffered ceiling creates the illusion of more headroom in the foyer; the architects enhanced all the ceilings with plaster moldings. The entertainment and dining halves of the family room are united by mahogany millwork. Kitchen cabinets pairing mahogany and tiger's-eye maple echo the family room's wainscoting; counters are Dumortierite. ➤

Clockwise from above: The daughter's bedroom. A new coffered ceiling, Calacatta marble fireplace, and walls handpainted in blue stripes distinguish the formal living room. Various marbles are employed in each of the home's three private bathrooms. Nafie designed built-in storage for every major room, including the son's bedroom; consistent panel detailing establishes continuity between painted and stained millwork. Mahogany media cabinets impart a library-like atmosphere in the family room.

PROJECT TEAM CHARLES J. NAFIE, AIA, CHRISTINA BATTISTON, AIDA MIRON, DANIEL BASKIN, NURALDIN SINGH
PHOTOGRAPHY JENNIFER FIORE

www.cjnaarchitects.com

2,600 sf
3 bedrooms, 3 ½ bathrooms

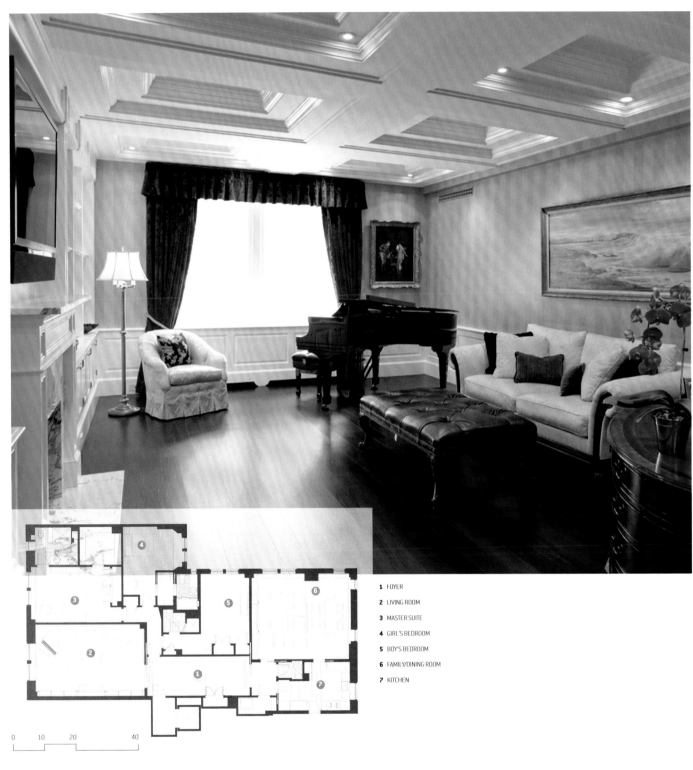

1 FOYER

2 LIVING ROOM

3 MASTER SUITE

4 GIRL'S BEDROOM

5 BOY'S BEDROOM

6 FAMILY/DINING ROOM

7 KITCHEN

0   10   20   40

Jaque Bethke for Pure Design Environments

THE CRIB
MINNETONKA, MINNESOTA

From below: A custom gas fireplace, made from a vintage rock-crushing machine filled with black granite, heats the patio. In the foyer, an Orleans area rug was custom cut into an eye shape to follow the curves of the painted Sheetrock soffits above. ➤

Until Jaque Bethke got a hold of it, this suburban home was a compartmentalized warren of small rooms. The designer opened up the layout to allow light in and augment the views out, transforming the cramped quarters into a fluid, streamlined space better suited to a contemporary lifestyle.

Bethke derived interior elements and millwork motifs—circles and squares positioned in novel configurations—from the geometry of the reworked floor plan. In the dining room, a round soffit highlighted by color-changing LEDs (programmable to more than 16 million shades) sets off a tree-trunk table surrounded by translucent acrylic chairs. Bold glass accents punctuate the warm smoky gray, royal purple, green, and bronze tones of the adjacent living area. Dark cherry and exotic Koto veneers combine with glass and stainless steel in the kitchen; the master suite exudes serenity and simplicity via taupes contrasted with deep gray woodwork and Carrara marble.

The exterior is equally dramatic, sporting a polished-limestone facade and copper roof accents. Decorative rain chains—wind-chime-like alternatives to humdrum closed-gutter downspouts—guide water to the ground, introducing a musical note to a functional element. Such attention to detail ensured that the Crib, as the home is affectionately called, would bring joy to the family within.

4,000 sf interior
2,000 sf patio
4 bedrooms, 5 ½ bathrooms

1 FOYER

2 DEN

3 GREAT ROOM

4 DINING AREA

5 KITCHEN

6 MASTER BEDROOM

7 MASTER BATHROOM

8 POWDER ROOM

9 MUDROOM

0   20   40   80

Clockwise from top left: *A street-art-influenced mural by Tamas "Zen One" Pomazi enlivens the children's bedroom; the custom beds have backlit acrylic headboards, and the pillows and hardware are accented with skulls and crossbones (inspired by fashion label Christian Audigier). The bathroom's handblown-glass chandelier was painstakingly assembled with 70 pieces. Copper rain chains are used in lieu of traditional spouts. Lights hidden in the stairwell's steel-tube divider creates an artistic effect by night. A geometric ceiling soffit perks up the gym. In the master suite, an Ultrasuede-upholstered bed designed by Jaque Bethke is detailed with crystal nail-heads. In the kitchen, warm-white flexible LEDs draw attention to the Fantasy Crusader backsplash tiles.*

DESIGN PRINCIPAL JAQUE BETHKE
PHOTOGRAPHY JILL GREER

www.jaquebethke.com

getaways

When designing a second
(or third or fourth) residence, homeowners
tend to venture into new waters. Whether said residence is an urban pied-à-terre, an island compound, a rural retreat, or a Deco-inspired luxury superyacht, clients typically indulge in fantasy, decadence, and bespoke detail. And they're often willing to embrace novel and sometimes experimental ways of living, with a heightened sense of openness and transparency and a desire to pare down (or, conversely, go extravagant). Hospitality-style amenities are de rigeur as well, from lavishly appointed decks to Jacuzzis and infinity-edge pools. *All aboard.*

Leverone Design

NOB HILL PIED-À-TERRE, SAN FRANCISCO

The owner of this compact San Francisco condo spends half the year here and the other half at his French countryside villa. Although the apartment was plenty serviceable for its pied-à-terre status, it lacked personality and, less forgivably, failed to capitalize on the enviable views of Grace Cathedral and Huntington Park.

Principal Matthew Leverone and his team took the reins, with six months to work their magic. Their first act was to reverse the locations of the dining and living spaces, moving the latter to the perimeter window wall. Now the balcony and stellar full-height views can be savored from the place where more time is spent, well, living. The dining room, meanwhile, was transformed into an intimate oak-paneled area. The paneling extends to the entry and kitchen, too, establishing continuity and warmth.

The firm prides itself on "tailored individuality, exquisite detail, and precise craftsmanship," and all three hallmarks are evident here. The interior has been simplified, in the kindest sense. From the tufted chaise to the leather-wrapped coffee table inspired by Jean-Michel Frank, each piece is designed so that the space reads as effortlessly uncluttered. And because neutrals dominate—gray, beige, white, rich wood finishes—accent colors have all the more impact: an orange throw here, a slate-blue chair there. A delicate and restrained touch is clearly at work.

From above: *A trio of benches in the living room are positioned to take in the panoramic cityscape. Beside a David Weeks light fixture, a custom daybed allows the guest room to function as a den as well; textiles and objects introduce a wealth of texture.* ⟶

1,100 sf
2 bedrooms, 2 bathrooms
Completed in 6 months

Clockwise from right:
An inviting armchair in the guest room beckons readers to a sunny spot. Oak-clad walls distinguish the dining area from the living area. Master bedroom walls are upholstered in wool; on the tufted-leather bed is a vintage Kuba-cloth pillow. A Gary Ruddell canvas in the dining room. A carved-wood Oromo stool injects levity in the master bedroom. Honed limestone tiles form the backdrop for refaced oak kitchen cabinets with white-bronze hardware. The bespoke partial-back chaise keeps sight lines unobstructed; the designers had the upholsterer custom-dye the thread to match the linen.

PROJECT TEAM MATTHEW LEVERONE, MICHELE STEDLEY, JOSÉ MAURÁS
PHOTOGRAPHY LISA ROMEREIN
www.leveronedesign.com

1 ENTRY

2 KITCHEN

3 LIVING AREA

4 DINING AREA

5 GUEST BEDROOM/DEN

6 MASTER BEDROOM

7 BATHROOM

0 5 10 20

155 feet long
5 cabins (10-guest capacity)
4 decks, wine cellar, and Jacuzzi

High design comes to the high seas via the M/Y *360°* luxury superyacht. Built in 2003 by renowned Italian shipyard ISA, the yacht was recently given a stately makeover by Yvonne Colacion. When the new owner approached the designer, the vessel was in dire need of an overhaul, despite coveted features like twin sweeping staircases, a clean-lined superstructure, and beautiful interior millwork. Bucking the industry trend to embrace either a hypermodern look or a staid traditional one, the team celebrated the glory days of yachting with a fresh take on the casual elegance of Art Deco luminaries Edgar Brandt and Émile-Jacques Ruhlmann.

Working from the outside in, the team visually adjusted window lines to lengthen the profile and obsessed over the perfect gray to enhance the all-white hull's graceful curves. Strategic contrasts helped define the interior quarters as well, creating the illusion of more space: Touches of ebony now accent the original medium-toned woodwork.

Colacion Studio vetted every material, finish, and furnishing for sturdiness and sensory response value, from the main salon's red-and-white wool carpet with accompanying zebra-print dining chairs to new built-ins and wenge blinds. Custom products and services were sourced from around the world, befitting a vessel that so artfully navigates the globe.

Colacion Studio

MOTOR YACHT *360°*

Clockwise from above: *In the main salon, macassar-frame chairs from Anne Hauck Art Deco are covered in Beacon Hill fabric; underfoot is a custom design from Decorative Carpets. Bespoke sofas from Ateliers Charles Jouffre are upholstered in a Rodolph fabric with Carnegie trim. A pair of curving staircases ascend from the bathing platform to the sundeck. The main staircase and lower-cabin hallway are floored in ebony. Colacion complemented the yacht's original built-in seating with dining chairs by Glyn Peter Machin.* ➥

Clockwise from above: Anne Hauck Art Deco tables and lounge chairs (covered in John Hutton fabric) gather in the observation lounge; the Trang console is by Applegate Tran. The captain's bridge. The observation lounge's custom wall-to-wall wool carpet, in a leopard pattern, is from Decorative Carpets. The 360° is at home on the sea. In the master suite, a Phoenix Day sconce illuminates a new headboard and built-in chest faced in ebony. The headboard and nightstand in the portside guest cabin are also bespoke; picture frame—like solid-wenge blinds throughout were provided by Ateliers Charles Jouffre.

PROJECT TEAM DESIGN PRINCIPAL: YVONNE COLACION, DESIGNER: KATHY TROUTFETTER
ARCHITECT/SHIPYARD ISA YACHTS
PHOTOGRAPHY ERIC LAIGNEL
www.colacionstudio.com

The Egg Design Group

WALKER'S POINT CONDOMINIUM, MILWAUKEE

A crackling fire, rough-hewn furnishings, a stunning sunset—what sounds like a woodsy vacation scene is actually set in an up-and-coming Milwaukee neighborhood called Walker's Point. Though rustic touches like vintage skis and a sheepskin throw suggest a secluded cabin, the design firm envisioned this 10th-floor condominium for a family eager to dive into the emerging cultural scene of the formerly industrial district.

With two of six children still at home, the family needed a space that could eventually transition from a weekend escape to an empty nest. The design is based on the Japanese principle of *wabi-sabi*, which embraces the beauty of imperfection and an aesthetic of asperity, asymmetry, and intimacy. Borrowing its palette from the skyline, the interior is a composition of textured earth tones and quiet grays. Chestnut-stained hardwood floors provide a warm counterpoint to metal accents, and vintage and contemporary lighting doubles as sculpture throughout.

Although the open-plan layout is ideal for entertaining, the home must also function for two high schoolers. The daughter's bedroom is furnished with custom art and a bubble chandelier, while the son's was designed to resemble his room at the family's primary home (consistency is important for those on the autism spectrum). The master suite includes a lounge, spalike bathroom, and panoramic views of the neighborhood. While the couple's life may get smaller in some ways when the kids head off to college, the world looks bigger than ever from here.

Clockwise from top:
A three-sided gas fireplace divides living and dining areas while preserving openness. In the dining area, a farm table with reclaimed chestnut top and metal base counters industrial views; the painting is by Timothy Meyerring. The kitchen works for family breakfasts and cocktail parties alike. In the master bedroom, gray tones complement the urban landscape; nightstands are vintage George Nelson cabinets and the chandelier is Murano mercury glass. ➤

3,090 sf
3 bedrooms, 3 ½ bathrooms

1 ENTRY FOYER

2 OFFICE

3 KITCHEN

4 DINING AREA

5 LIVING AREA

6 MASTER SUITE

7 BEDROOM

Clockwise from left:
In the entryway, an
industrial cabinet,
Foscarini Gregg
pendant, and vintage
Adami print set a
sleek tone. The son's
bedroom features
an Eames desk,
an Emeco 111 Navy
chair made from
recycled plastic
Coke bottles, a Louis
Poulsen floor lamp,
and vintage aviation
photography. A
Sticotti shelf-and-
desk unit creates an
urban office space.
The master bedroom
and sitting area are
furnished in shades
of mink. A bubble
chandelier crowns
the daughter's room.

DESIGN PRINCIPAL LYNN TARRENCE
PHOTOGRAPHY TRICIA SHAY
www.theeggdesigngroup.com

Philpotts Interiors

ISLAND RETREAT, MANELE BAY, LANAI, HAWAII

Clockwise from top:
Slate roof tile was
selected for its
likeness to lava stone.
The designer crowned
a found cabinet with
a stone counter and
vessel to create a
vanity. In the pool
hale, teak and wicker
finishes, salvaged-
wood tabletops, and
columns of carved
ohia tree trunks echo
the surroundings.
Pigmented plaster
and a custom
headboard carved in
Bali add texture to a
guest bedroom. ➥

This oceanfront vacation house for a California-based artist and her family consists of three plantation-style pavilions with retractable walls, ohia trunk columns, and alfresco walkways carpeted in grass. Marion Philpotts-Miller followed the palette of Hawaii's natural surroundings in choosing warm, vibrant colors for the inside, too. In the great room, cabana stripes in orange, red, and cream cover cushions on teak chairs. Like tall birds-of-paradise, floor lamps shaded in crimson flank a wood daybed festooned with pillows in an array of patterns and fiery hues; in guest bedrooms, lively lime and ochre walls lighten the generous dose of wood. The master suite is dressed in neutrals; stronger colors are provided by the ever-evolving views of ocean and sky.

Teak and lava stone may be part of the island vernacular, but the design firm—which has operated offices in both San Francisco and Honolulu for two decades—sourced tradesmen elsewhere because of the project's isolated location and tight budget. Artisans in Bali carved headboards to look like Chinese folding screens. Vintage metal-mesh patio chairs with a perfectly weathered patina were picked up in the Bay Area. And Tilevera in Sausalito reinterpreted a textile to create the kitchen's custom blue-and-white backsplash. In the end, the remote location paid off: Traditional Hawaiian architecture meets a modern mix.

Floor plan legend:

1 ENTRY LANAI

2 KITCHEN

3 GREAT ROOM

4 OFFICE

5 MASTER BATHROOM

6 MASTER BEDROOM

7 POOL HALE

8,700 sf
4 bedrooms,
4 ½ baths

DESIGN PRINCIPAL MARION PHILPOTTS-MILLER, ASID, IIDA
ARCHITECT SHAY ZAK/ZAK ARCHITECTURE
PHOTOGRAPHY MATTHEW MILLMAN
www.philpotts.net

Clockwise from opposite: In the main pavilion, vibrant weatherproof textiles were specified from Perennials; the pendants over the dining table are from Roost in Sausalito. Mellow tones prevail in the master bedroom; beyond, the pool glows at the edge of a cliff. The downward-sloping site allows for astounding views from the entry lanai. Reclaimed teak panels, once a gate, were assembled into a guest room headboard.

Vanessa Deleon Associates

PRIVATE APARTMENT, NEW YORK

Clockwise from right:
In an alcove between the dining room and sitting area, a life-size statue is poised to take in the view. The living room is furnished with a Tui Lifestyle leather sleeper, a wool-and-silk shag rug from the Rug Importer, and an M16 Rifle floor lamp by Philippe Starck. The entry hall is treated to a custom mosaic from Sicis. The open-plan kitchen features a stainless-steel cooking surface and cabinetry, an island with rolling cart, and a pantry enclosed in etched glass. Wenge-and-marble shelving by Molteni & C gives the office area an architectural edge. The building exterior.

The Chelsea neighborhood of Manhattan has seen some major architectural additions of late—Polshek Partnership's topsy-turvy Standard Hotel, Neil Denari's elegantly swoopy HL23—but none is as accomplished as 100 11th Avenue, by French powerhouse Jean Nouvel. The building's astonishing curtain wall is a curving network of 1,650 colorless-glass windowpanes, each set at a different angle and torque to create a striking avant-garde exterior.

So what to do with the interior, specifically an apartment on a high floor? "You have to honor the integrity of Nouvel's vision," explains Vanessa Deleon. Luckily, her globe-trotting bachelor client agreed. Deleon kept the design modern and sleek, echoing the faceted exterior with a bespoke mosaic in the entry hall. Custom remote-controlled window shades of various colors and widths, similarly recalling the geometric facade, modulate the enviable city views. Pops of green enliven the classic black-and-white palette, as does an Asian-style statue standing in the nook between dining and living areas. Contributing panache is a mix of furnishings by renowned designers: Philippe Starck, Mies van der Rohe, and—natch—Nouvel himself.

DESIGN PRINCIPAL VANESSA DELEON
PHOTOGRAPHY ANTONY BIANCIELLA
www.vanessadeleon.com

610 sf
$500,000 budget
3 bedrooms, 3 bathrooms

Figamma

FINANCIAL DISTRICT APARTMENT, NEW YORK

Clockwise from above: *The master bedroom incorporates a study. Figamma accented the larger of two guest rooms with vibrant red paint; Jasper Morrison Glo-Ball lamps sit atop the bedside tables. Swiveling panels between the sleeping and bathing areas allow for soaks with a view.* ➤

Open-plan, loft-style arrangements aren't for everyone. At least, not for this Bogotá-based firm's longtime client, a globe-trotting businessman with two grown children and frequent guests. Figamma steered the client away from the studio he'd initially selected for his Manhattan pied-à-terre, suggesting instead a nuclear multi-bedroom layout that could more graciously host visitors and gatherings.

To get ample square footage, the designers joined two apartments, both located on the 36th floor of a downtown high-rise with spectacular Hudson River views. The newly formed three-bedroom had less advantageous attributes, too; namely, a tricky acute-angled window wall in the living/dining area. Custom silk-and-wool area rugs help soften the angularity and delineate the space, while top-of-the-line AV equipment offers ample distractions. Simple and sophisticated furnishings were selected from a roster of edgy Italian labels: Minotti, Poltrona Frau, Natuzzi, de Sede. Leather, high-touch textiles, wood, colored glass, and warm metals provide rich accents, as do gypsum tapestries fabricated by Colombian artisans.

A wet bar–like concealed kitchen in the living area allows for easy entertaining. Walk-in closets in all three bedrooms are sure to accommodate whatever baggage a houseful of guests can provide. And when the host needs some quiet time, he can retreat to the private lounge in his master suite.

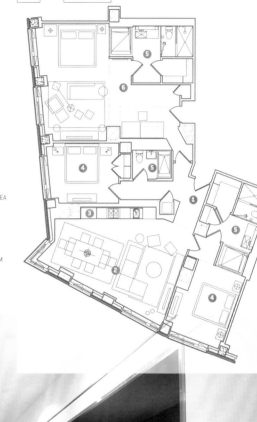

Clockwise from top left: The master bedroom has a private lounge area with top-of-the-line Bang & Olufsen AV equipment. Subway tile clads the en suite master bathroom. Sliding panels can be closed to hide the kitchen from the triangular living/dining area. Yellow dominates the smaller guest room.

0   5   10   20

PROJECT TEAM LINA MARIA GONZÁLEZ, FERNANDO GONZÁLEZ, LUZ PIEDAD SANTA
PHOTOGRAPHY JUAN FELIPE RUBIO

www.figamma.com

1 ENTRY

2 LIVING/DINING AREA

3 KITCHEN

4 GUEST ROOM

5 BATHROOM

6 MASTER BEDROOM

BT Arquitectos

BLUE BAHIA, PANAMA CITY

Clockwise from above: *In the living/dining area, backlit alabaster cladding the core acts as a giant light fixture while uniting the colors of the furniture and other finishes. The stone slabs, which were sourced in Spain, guide visitors beyond the foyer stairway to the living area. In the master bedroom, a textural wall provides a restful counterpoint to the bright and sleek common spaces.*

If empty nesters are known for overhauling their homes, then this project in Panama City's glitzy Punta Pacifica neighborhood exemplifies that transformation. With two kids off to college, a successful businessman and his wife tapped local architects David Bettis and Teófilo Tarazi to convert their large apartment into a luxurious party venue for cocktails and dinner parties.

The bi-level residence is located near the top of a new 41-story condo tower, and its renovation was completed just two years after the opening of the building itself. Yet the client spared no expense in the name of entertainment. The generous budget allowed BT Arquitectos to replace the existing stairway near the entry with a custom creation whose glass-and-steel palette underscores the apartment's sky-high location. Visitors pass the steps to deposit themselves in the double-height living area that BT combined with the dining room to maximize capacity. The highlight of this social space is another bespoke fabrication: a backlit alabaster wall. The translucent stone also lines the foyer and a mezzanine seating area; the visual continuity encourages guests to fan out and up. The curious among them will also discover that parenting remains a priority in this household: In addition to the master suite, two spare bedrooms await visiting offspring.

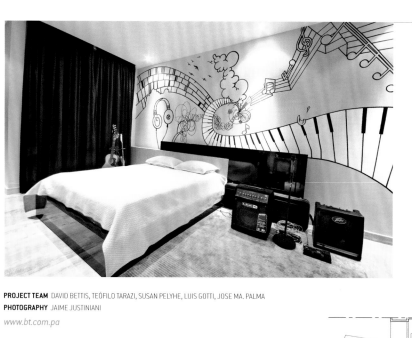

4,040 sf
$600,000 budget

PROJECT TEAM DAVID BETTIS, TEÓFILO TARAZI, SUSAN PELYHE, LUIS GOTTI, JOSE MA. PALMA
PHOTOGRAPHY JAIME JUSTINIANI

www.bt.com.pa

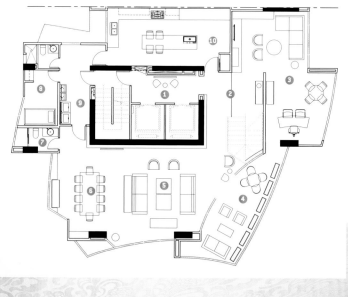

0   10   20   40

1 LOBBY
2 FOYER
3 FAMILY ROOM/STUDY
4 BALCONY
5 LIVING AREA
6 DINING AREA
7 POWDER ROOM
8 MAID'S SUITE
9 LAUNDRY ROOM
10 KITCHEN

Clockwise from above: The foyer staircase was fabricated in Bogotá. A wood-ensconced lounge is tucked behind the stairwell on the upper level. Generous seating on the balcony adjacent to the living area allows partygoers to venture outside. In the family room/office— as elsewhere— seating space was optimized. Juan Davis was commissioned to paint a festive mural for a guest bedroom's headboard wall.

green

With the surge in new earth-conscious finishes, products, and systems, more people are rising to the challenge of building green.

Sustainability takes many shapes in the following projects, from an off-the-grid, net-zero-energy beachfront retreat and a LEED-certified wine-country dwelling to downtown lofts that pay homage to all things recycled, reclaimed, and repurposed. Many make optimal use of natural light and rare breezes, address the demands of the land and ecosystems, integrate ecofriendly materials, employ vegetative roofs and solar power collecting, and/or blur the boundaries between inside and out. They achieve natural beauty while leaving the lightest footprint possible. *Step inside.*

Heliotrope Architects

NORTH BEACH RESIDENCE, ORCAS ISLAND, WASHINGTON

Interior Design Hall of Fame member Rysia Suchecka had summered for nearly 30 years on this rugged island with her environmental-engineer husband, John Warburton, and wanted an upgrade from their prefab cabin. The couple's brief to architect Joseph Herrin called for a low-impact, durable, and easy-to-maintain structure that tread lightly on—and engaged with—the land it occupies.

Overlooking the Strait of Georgia, the beachfront site boasts second-growth Douglas firs, a beech grove, and a grassy meadow. For more than a millennium, it served Lummi Indians as a winter encampment; thus the site's archaeological significance ruled out foundation excavation. In addition, the land was in a federally designated flood plain so the house would need to be elevated several feet.

Herrin carefully nestled the lean I-shape structure among the trees, erecting full-height glass walls that open directly onto the beach and meadow. To avoid excavation, a mat slab was poured right over the grass, and the foundation recessed to minimize the building's footprint. The elemental form fairly floats, so as not to disturb the groundwater flow. A green roof further reduces stormwater runoff—captured and reused for irrigation and flushing toilets—and creates a rich habitat for insects. Solar collectors and PV panels provide much of the electricity. But for all its ecofriendly credentials, the design is first and foremost a comfortable haven for communing with nature.

Clockwise from below: *The metal-clad structure was sited to minimize disturbance to existing Douglas firs: No trees were removed during construction. A built-in bookcase in the living room forms a fireplace surround; Suchecka designed most of the furniture and had many pieces built by an island cabinet-maker. A double vanity housed in the master bedroom rests on alder flooring.* ➤

Clockwise from above: *The house, as seen from the beach. A view from the master bedroom to one of two guest bedrooms, accessed via a door off the deck. Suchecka, who uses a guest bedroom as her office, can take in sunsets through a sliver window. The main refrigerator-freezer is housed in the pantry. A pair of mirror-image guest bedrooms caps one end of the house; each has its own WC but shares the double shower between them. The glassed-in master bathroom.*

DESIGN PRINCIPAL JOSEPH HERRIN
INTERIOR DESIGN RYSIA SUCHECKA
PHOTOGRAPHY SEAN AIRHART

www.heliotropearchitects.com

2,070 sf
3 bedrooms, 3 bathrooms
Sustainable attributes include a vegetated roof plus hot-water and hydronic heating aided with solar collectors and PV panels

1 LIVING AREA
2 DINING AREA
3 KITCHEN
4 PANTRY
5 WARDROBE
6 MASTER SUITE
7 GUEST BEDROOM
8 GUEST SHOWER

0   10   20   40

Roth Kimura

8,139 sf interior
2,795 sf lanai
4 bedrooms, 7 bathrooms

As befits a home located in the South Seas paradise of Hawaii, this airy, light-filled residence is designed to bring the outside in. All major rooms open onto lush tropical grounds, and each bedroom connects to its own serene courtyard. The house is an assembly of pavilions set along paths that wend their way to a pool boasting striking Haleakala volcano and ocean views. Nearby, waiting to be discovered, are life-size bronze A'ama crabs hiding in the rocks and a magnificent whale's tail sculpture by artist Gloria Bornstein. These are just some of the artisanal details that invite a further look; one-of-a-kind light sconces by Gerald Ben and custom doors carved by Jeera Rattanangkul also add bespoke detail.

Soaring skylit ceilings lend cathedral presence to the great room and welcome in Wakea, the Sky Father. The loftlike space is divided into intimate seating vignettes, a wise choice that allows outsize proportions to coexist with cozy nooks for nestling. State-of-the-art energy-saving technologies are used throughout the property: Photovoltaic panels capture solar energy, and the heat generated by air conditioners warms the water supply and swimming pool. This sense of environmental responsibility enhances the stylish residence, which marries grandeur and homeyness with ease.

Clockwise from opposite: The sun-soaked great room, which features a vaulted timber ceiling, connects to the lanai and a palm-fringed garden overlooking the ocean. Even the foyer walkway has stunning sea views. Light streams in through horizontal glass panels in the upstairs hallway. The welcoming entrance. ➤

DESIGN PRINCIPAL JUSTINE STERLING
PHOTOGRAPHY STUART SIEGEL

www.justinesterling.com

3,700 sf
4 bedrooms, 3 bathrooms

Issi Design

JINMAO VILLA, SHANGHAI, CHINA

Modern-day Shanghai is distinguished by a hodgepodge of architectural vintages and genres. But among the most iconic—and beautiful—buildings are the recently revamped turn-of-the-century Art Deco and neoclassical banks that populate the Bund, the city's waterfront district. Issi Design exported this Old Shanghai vernacular to a countryside vacation villa for a local businessman who coveted the style.

In China, speculative developers deliver concrete-block shells to homeowners who design them as they wish. In the case of Jinmao Villa, soaring public spaces intended for a Mediterranean decor proved equally suited to fluted marble walls, coffered ceilings, and other Gatsby-era motifs.

But the original architect had not considered that the client would be hosting business associates in addition to housing his wife and two teenage children. To secure privacy for all parties, creative director Andy Leung inserted two en suite bedrooms at opposite ends of the ground floor—clearly removed from the four bedrooms upstairs.

Another adaptation was to elevate the importance of basement spaces where mah-jongg games and other group activities would occur. (The house also boasts a home theater, spa, billiard room, and gym.) Leung minimized nonstructural partitions between these subterranean rooms and illuminated them in a rhythmic fashion, suggesting daylight flowing through windows. A bright idea indeed.

Clockwise from above: An Art Deco bas-relief makes a bold statement in the marble-lined foyer. A dog statuette in the master bedroom symbolizes good fortune. In the living room, pilasters and flutes carved into the fireplace wall enhance the loftlike sense of volume. ➤

7,500 sf
2 kitchens,
4 bedrooms,
6 bathrooms

DESIGN PRINCIPAL/CREATIVE DIRECTOR ANDY LEUNG
ARCHITECTURE EDACI
PHOTOGRAPHY NACASA & PARTNERS

www.issi-design.com

1 GARAGE
2 ENTRY FOYER
3 LIVING ROOM
4 KITCHEN
5 DINING ROOM
6 MUSIC ROOM
7 TERRACE
8 GUEST SUITE
9 OFFICE

0   20   40   80

Clockwise from right: In the master bedroom, fluting and reeding on the mahogany headboard wall echo the folds of the curtains. Cork wallpaper clads the music corner adjacent to the formal dining room. The master bedroom's walk-in closet includes a leisure space enveloped in leather and copper; the dressing area features wardrobe doors, a built-in vanity, and a jewelry vitrine— all mahogany. In addition to communal entertainment rooms, the basement level houses an exercise room and spa. In the family room, a copper accent wall reflects a lighting plan that emphasizes variety over uniformity.

Therese Virserius Design

TUDOR CITY APARTMENT, NEW YORK

"A welcoming, luxury-hotel experience" is how the clients described their vision for their fourth residence: a pied-à-terre in Tudor City, built in the 1920s and billed as the world's first residential skyscraper complex. Therese Virserius tapped into her hospitality background to envision a design at once worldly and homey. In her quest to deliver a more open layout, the antiquated unit was gutted down to the studs and framing. The designer then installed limewashed wide-plank oak flooring throughout, eschewing saddles to enhance the sense of flow.

A quietly dynamic color palette creates hushed drama and continuity. Soft lavender tones in the living room segue to muted champagne in the bedrooms, while the kitchen's custom cabinetry is a sleek mix of whitewashed oak and gloss-painted white. Furnishings, too, possess an airy quality and many—such as Eva Zeisel's playful glass-top coffee table—have sculptural profiles. Vignettes are anchored by a selection of darker, weightier pieces: Leggy obsidian-hued chairs encircling a round table delineate the dining space; black lamps on Hans Sandgren Jakobsen side tables flank a custom living room sofa. Breezy sheers reiterate the free-flowing vibe.

The urbane getaway has all the grace of a pedigreed European hotel. And luckily for the clients, they never have to check out.

900 sf
2 bedrooms

DESIGN PRINCIPAL THERESE VIRSERIUS
PHOTOGRAPHY ANDREAS KORNFELD

www.theresevirseriusdesign.com

Eileen Dycus
By Design

PRUITT HOUSE, MOORESTOWN, NEW JERSEY

Eileen Dycus has a motto: Go big or stay home. Or in the case of her work for the Pruitts, an active family with two daughters, Go bigger *at* home. The couple commissioned the designer to add a new kitchen, family room, and wraparound deck, convert their existing kitchen into a back foyer, and expand the basement—more than doubling the footprint. "I masterminded everything from the overarching concept and the architectural renderings down to the most minute details," Dycus explains of her hands-on approach, "and I oversaw every single phase of construction."

Big changes require big ideas, and Dycus had a number of them. She lifted the ceilings, which were 8 feet in the original portion of the house, to 9 feet in the new kitchen and 12 in the family room. Furnishing the latter are numerous custom pieces, handcrafted in Italy using salvaged antique woods; even the fireplace surround was made with 250-year-old Italian chestnut. To complement the copious millwork, she deployed luxurious fabrics.

Dycus saved her best moves for the kitchen, however. A formidable island stands at its center; above is a cupola decorated with commissioned nature-scene paintings and topped with an 18th-century panel from France; a trio of glittering chandeliers descends through the open coffers.

Those coffers proved the greatest challenge: Schedule restraints and sample snafus left little time to install them. Undaunted, Dycus enlisted the help of her family and spent a week between Christmas and New Year's hand-staining over 4,700 linear feet of millwork for said ceilings and that magnificent cupola, earning big cheers—and gratitude—from her clients.

Clockwise from near right: The ornate door and windows meet Energy Star ratings; the new deck is 1,500 square feet. In the foyer and throughout, Dycus specified an eclectic mix of flora— both true and faux— from Petals & Blooms and NDI. Rich woods and fine antiques predominate. ➤

"My work is a by-product of strong relationships developed with clients, and it blossoms when I'm granted full trust to envision their dreams" —EILEEN DYCUS

Clockwise from top left: A commissioned painting by Kyle Confehr hangs over the family room's custom fireplace surround and mantel, fabricated by Artitalia Group in Italy. A blend of old (antiques) and new (fresh-cut flowers) offers a lively contrast. Ample sunlight and Energy Star–rated radiant subfloor heating warm the house. A custom daybed in the informal dining/sunroom provides a perfect showcase for a painting the clients collected from Dycus's gallery. Hickory White chairs surround the Fremarc Designs custom dining table. ➤

Grand coffers—hand-stained by Dycus herself—grace the family room. The custom armoire, dual-drawer console, and flip-top table in the sitting area were crafted by Artitalia Group with reclaimed antique woods. Pearson Furniture leather sofas and custom down seating join Hickory White damask lounge chairs and an arched-back reading chair, all sitting on a custom Kravet rug. The rose-print fabric on the dining chairs is a bespoke design from Andrew Martin. The chandeliers and lamps are by Currey & Co.

1,150 sf new construction
140 sf reconstruction
1,500 sf new deck
7,800 linear feet new millwork

1 FAMILY ROOM

2 BREAKFAST ROOM

3 KITCHEN

4 BACK FOYER

5 DECK

6 COVERED DECK

0   5   10   20

DESIGN PRINCIPAL EILEEN DYCUS
BUILDER BARTA BUILDERS/EILEEN DYCUS
DECK CONSTRUCTION ABBOTT CONSTRUCTION
GRANITE FABRICATION SAM MARINI/INTELCO
IRONWORK BOB SIMS
DRAPERY WORKROOM BLAGICA DIMISKOVSKI/DRAPERY WORKS
PHOTOGRAPHY GARRETT ROWLAND

www.eileendycus.com

Clockwise from top left: The handcrafted kitchen cabinetry, which pairs antique mappa burl and reclaimed wood, was treated to water- and plant-based stains; the design is part of Dycus's custom line, manufactured by Artitalia Group. The reproduction flip-top desk, also made of antique wood, is a custom piece by Scott Thomas. Above the zebrawood kitchen island, topped with Golden Flake/Black Galaxy granite, chandeliers descend from the art-filled cupola. Artichokes spill from a vintage bucket. McKinley Leather designed the turned-leg armchair near the family room's Isokern fireplace.

Dexter Dyer Design

LAGUNA BEACH HOUSE, CALIFORNIA

The weathered textures of driftwood and beach glass influenced the design of this airy house, giving it the appearance of a decades-old bungalow—not the rebuilt teardown that it is. The owners purchased the property after renting it one summer, so were well acquainted with both its pros (location, location, location) and cons, namely decrepitude and a hopelessly outdated 1930s decor.

They hired Dexter Dyer Design to envision a simple, manageable structure that took best advantage of the sloped site and ocean view. A low roofline gives the illusion of a small one-story, but inside, the house lives large— a feeling enhanced by generous decks and patios. The master suite is on the main floor to facilitate unilevel living when the couple is solo; for overnight guests, there's a fully contained lower level boasting a bistro kitchen, two sleeping suites, and a family room. Also on this floor is an art studio with storage that lets the client, who sometimes hosts classes, stash painting materials out of sight when the house is in entertaining mode.

Extensive woodwork lends a cozy feel top to bottom, from the coffered Douglas fir ceilings to the French oak flooring. Scaled-down furnishings maximize square footage and salvaged pieces—such as the Indonesian spice cabinet repurposed as a vanity and a cotton trolley reborn as a coffee table—honor the vintage, beachy vibe.

Clockwise from right: *The linen slipcover on the living room's custom sofa is forgiving—it has been treated to resist stains. Vintage host chairs bookend a distressed-wood dining table with industrial base. Dark-stained millwork in a guest bath contrasts with light stone and wood. Cream trim gives lift to the house, shingled in two patterns; the deck, accessible from the master bedroom and living room, wraps all the way around the house.* ⤵

2,900 sf
3 bedrooms,
3½ bathrooms

1 ENTRY

2 DINING AREA

3 KITCHEN

4 GREAT ROOM

5 DECK

6 MASTER SUITE

7 GARAGE

8 LAUNDRY ROOM

9 POWDER ROOM

0   10   20   40

Clockwise from near right: Fretwork frames on the master bath's mirror disguise medicine cabinets. The kitchen system is by SieMatic. Deep cornice boxes conceal motorized roller shades in the master bedroom (and throughout), where a custom bed is covered in Kravet stripes. The custom bookcase/media cabinet in the lower-level family room received a sandblasted and wire-brushed finish that mimics driftwood. Surrounded by Bausman & Company chairs, the breakfast table serves as a bridge table, too: The clients are avid players.

DESIGN PRINCIPAL DEXTER DYER
ARCHITECT OF RECORD BRION JEANNETTE ARCHITECTURE
BUILDER BUWALDA CONSTRUCTION
PHOTOGRAPHY ANDREW R. ABRECHT
www.dexterdyerdesign.com

global inspiration

Some people return from world travels with a suitcase full of souvenirs; others arrive back home stoked with fresh design inspiration. These globe-trotting couples and intrepid families fall squarely into the latter category. Their far-flung connections—places of origin, places they've visited or lived—provide fodder for a major makeover or a brand-new home. The result? Cultural touchstones cropping up in unexpected places. An Italian countryside villa...on Lake Michigan. South African style...on the Upper East Side. Balinese mindfulness and spiritualism...in Hawaii. (And in Los Angeles, too.) And the tongue-in-cheek exoticism of Turkish opium dens...in Puerto Rico. *Around the world—and back again.*

Philpotts Interiors

BEACH HOUSE WITH SPIRIT
KAHUKU, OAHU, HAWAII

Falling in love with a place on vacation is one thing; re-creating the magic close to home is quite another. On a visit to Bali, this family was so taken with the island's serene and mindful atmosphere, they hired Marion Philpotts-Miller to design a home on Hawaii's North Shore that expressed that affinity. The challenge was to preserve the sense of spirituality while modernizing it—and tailoring it to family life.

At the entry, a Balinese *angkul-angkul* gateway links the garage and driveway to an inner courtyard while serving as a buffer against North Shore winds. Beyond is a dramatically lit traditional water feature, complete with a gong for announcing guests. Numerous areas beckon you to enjoy the tropical climate: There's a traditional *bale* pavilion with a terracotta crown roof, a vast lawn with teak chaises and a fire bowl, and an infinity pool set off with Hawaiian naupaka plantings.

The interior has its charms, of course—particularly the master suite, whose raised sleeping platform offers spectacular ocean views. Everywhere are treasures acquired on the fabled trip, among them a teak pedestal table, a custom ebony console, and countless stone gods. And even entering the garden bath, with its *ofuro* soaking tub presided over by antique Buddha's heads, is like stepping through a door into Bali.

Clockwise from top:
The view from the infinity pool. In the living area, fans with oil-rubbed bronze palm-leaf blades circulate air; the high ceilings are clad in bamboo, which helps keep things cool. ➤

13,415 sf
5 bedrooms,
6½ bathrooms

1 ENTRY

2 OFFICE

3 DINING AREA

4 LIVING AREA

5 KITCHEN

6 BEDROOM

7 MASTER SUITE

8 PATIO

9 POOL

10 POOL HOUSE

0 10 20 40

DESIGN PRINCIPAL MARION PHILPOTTS-MILLER, ASID, IIDA
ARCHITECT WILLIAM J. HIRSH JR.
PHOTOGRAPHY ART GRAY

www.philpotts.net

Clockwise from opposite top: The kitchen features a rustic copper range hood, custom cabinetry with woven panels, and pendants that replicate candlelight. Philpotts-Miller topped the master-suite bed with a contemporary take on the kapa mua, a traditional Hawaiian quilt. A venerable Buddha's head presides over the garden bath's Japanese soaking tub. A teak-and-cane lazy chair sourced in Bali warms the tempera-finished travertine flooring in a bedroom. The Bali trip also yielded the living area's coffee table, topped in a slab of Albizia saman.

3,630 sf
4 bedrooms, 3 ½ baths

Kellie Smith
Design Studio

GEORGIAN REVIVAL HOME
DALTON, GEORGIA

When Kellie Smith was hired to revamp this 1930s Georgian-style home, the mission was to incorporate contemporary touches while honoring the structure's original character. During weekly shopping trips, the designer encouraged her clients to "buy what they loved," integrating their finds into the overall scheme to create a uniquely personal space. The globe-trotting couple also wanted to incorporate pieces from their travels, found objects, and family heirlooms—all from different periods. Smith mixed these styles seamlessly, layering the space with warmth and color. In the living room, for instance, a translucent Philippe Starck Ghost chair that nods to Louis XV is paired with a more traditional secretary desk.

But to acknowledge the classic roots of the home, some modifications were more subtle: In the library, which—thankfully—retained its vintage mahogany paneling, 1960s-era bookshelves were refaced with complementing antiqued trim. Conjoining centuries of decor wasn't the project's only unification challenge, either; Smith also reworked a disjointed layout, the result of renovations done over the decades.

The newlyweds love their new home. Whenever they return from traveling, they're welcomed by their private oasis: a well-designed space that truly reflects them.

Clockwise from above: The living room mixes family heirlooms with contemporary finishes; the fireplace surround is clad in stainless-steel tiles. The mahogany-paneled library. A Juju headdress from Cameroon takes pride of place in the living room. The powder room features glass mosaic tiles, a bronze sink, and artisan-painted walls. A traditional secretary desk is updated in cerulean. The bedroom fireplace was rebuilt in rough-cut golden onyx and travertine, which pop against dramatic charcoal walls and bursts of crimson upholstery.

DESIGN PRINCIPAL KELLIE SMITH
PHOTOGRAPHY MELANIE SUGGS
www.kelliesmithdesignstudio.com

Tracie Butler Interior Design

MARMONT PROJECT, LOS ANGELES

The Hollywood Hills is a location that conjures filmic glamour: winding Mulholland Drive with its wide-angle city vistas rendered in flattering soft focus by atmospheric smog, Spanish-style villas decorated in Hollywood Regency chic, modernist cubes tricked out as bachelor playgrounds for hermetic millionaires. It's a seductive scene, for sure, but is it also a little...cliché, perhaps?

There's nothing of the West Coast razzle-dazzle about this house, which takes cues instead from serene Balinese interiors. The project was designed from the ground up for a businessman with a fondness for the Far East. Natural materials are key to the decor, providing layers of texture. Ruched silk and pony-hair wall coverings bedeck the master suite, draperies are fashioned from hemp and linen, and organic grass cloth is used throughout. Walnut and teak finishes imbued with great sheen and depth characterize the floors and walls, and Indonesian artifacts exist amid the jewel-tone colors that punctuate the otherwise streamlined environment.

"The motivation for this project was to create a harmonic relationship between space and energy," says Tracie Butler, whose intuitive approach eschews slavish devotion to any one set of design rules. Safe to say, mission accomplished.

Clockwise from below: The three-sided hearth has a niche for firewood; Balinese statues reflect the Indonesian theme. A mosaic-tiled pool provides respite from the California sun. A Roman Coin panel by ecofriendly manufacturer Livinglass brings light to the second-floor overlook. The same material faces cabinet doors; river rocks are embedded in the poured-resin dining-table top. A floating staircase bridges levels. ➤

4,500 sf
4 bedrooms, 4 bathrooms

1 GARAGE

2 ENTRY FOYER

3 KITCHEN

4 DINING AREA

5 LIVING ROOM

6 DEN

7 MEDIA ROOM

8 BATHROOM

0   10   20   40

DESIGN PRINCIPAL TRACIE BUTLER
ARCHITECT OF RECORD (FER) STUDIO
PHOTOGRAPHY VAL RIOLO

www.traciebutlerdesign.com

Clockwise from above: *Handcrafted furniture in the living area gets a jolt from vivid colors. Exotic stones line the shower walls of the guest bathroom. Hand-carved rock-crystal lamps and a leather headboard set a cool tone in the master bedroom. The pillowed onyx tiles, marble floor, and skylit walk-in shower are standout features in the master bath. Limestone paves the patio, and low-slung furniture plays host to pillows and cushions in fabrics by Perennials, Kravet, and Rose Tarlow Melrose House. Screening the shower in the master bath is a walnut-framed, smoked-glass mirror that mimics the doorway to the sleeping area.*

4,200 sf
4 bedrooms, 4 bathrooms

Jeffrey Beers
International

CENTRAL PARK WEST RESIDENCE
NEW YORK

The location was peerless: 15 Central Park West, the luxe condo tower designed by Robert A. M. Stern. So how could this lily be gilded? The client, originally from South Africa, has an affinity for art and travel. Jeffrey Beers envisioned the space she shared with her children as an open, sunlit modern loft suitable for entertaining and displaying her collection of contemporary paintings and sculptures. Achieving that goal required rethinking the existing floor plan, fixtures, and finishes to devise something more in keeping with the client's aesthetic.

Beers heightened the impact of the windows and natural light, creating a canvas for visually dynamic artworks. Rich with elements that speak to South African culture, the interior scheme emphasizes texture, material, and color. The palette is largely neutral with judicious pops of warm orange and cool blue. To instill a sense of grandeur in the otherwise streamlined, loftlike environment, Beers used 12-inch-wide white-oak plank floors throughout and large slabs of silver travertine in the master bath. Hand-rubbed plaster finishes, antique cement tiles, ivory leather wall panels, and doors veneered with smoked European oak add a warm, homey dimension that keeps the decor from tipping toward austere.

Clockwise from top:
In the foyer, a screen of glass roundels funnels light from the dining area beyond. Central Park views and a beamed ceiling dominate the living room, a multipurpose relaxation and entertainment hub. The living room's low-slung club chairs pull up to a custom glass-top table. Handblown pendant fixtures, a chainsaw-textured solid-oak table with cast-bronze base, and leather-wrapped chairs lend the dining area a downtown sensibility—with uptown polish. ➤

Clockwise from top left: *The powder-room walls were treated to a hand-rubbed plaster finish. Organic hues distinguish the master bedroom. A colorful vintage Egg chair perks up a secondary bedroom; the headboard is upholstered in a Hella Jongerius print. In the kitchen, solid zebrawood composes the island countertop and open shelving. The striations of the master bath's silver travertine slabs deftly echo the grain of the kitchen's zebrawood.*

1	ENTRY
2	MASTER SUITE
3	LIBRARY
4	LIVING AREA
5	DINING AREA
6	KITCHEN
7	BEDROOM
8	MEDIA ROOM
9	POWDER ROOM

PROJECT TEAM JEFFREY BEERS, EDWARD
ACERO, NORA KANTER, MASAKO FUKUOKA
PHOTOGRAPHY PETER PAIGE

www.jeffreybeers.com

2,500 sf
2 bedrooms, 2 bathrooms

Therese Virserius Design

CHELSEA LOFT, NEW YORK

Therese Virserius leads a boutique firm that tackles hospitality and residential projects around the globe. This design project, however, brought her home: to her own living space in Manhattan. A bare loft in the arty Chelsea neighborhood provided the perfect canvas—after adding plumbing, electricity, and interior walls, that is.

Virserius's goal was to create a calm and relaxing dwelling amenable to entertaining. She accomplished the latter by leaving the kitchen and living room open to each other, establishing a social hub. Friends can congregate around the cooking island during parties; wheels allow for maneuvering it out of the way when more floor space is called for. Serenity comes via the predominance of soothing gray tones, dark ipe flooring, and the gallerylike installation of meaningful sculptures and photography.

Private quarters are kept tucked away from the main space. There's a secluded master suite complete with a spa tub, a guest bedroom with en suite bathroom, and an extensive library well appointed with several hundred books on subjects ranging from geography and finance to philosophy and, of course, design.

DESIGN PRINCIPAL THERESE VISERIUS
PHOTOGRAPHY THERESE VISERIUS
www.theresevirseriusdesign.com

Clockwise from right:
The loft's open living area is furnished with a worldly mix of custom pieces accumulated on the designer's travels; Shanghai was the inspiration for the lounges' floral fabric. A raku installation by sculptor Joe Conforti enlivens one column. Anchoring the dining area is a commissioned photograph of the New York skyline at night by artist Regina Virserius, the designer's sister. The foyer is defined by a 500-pound abstract sculpture in carved Carrara marble by Ken Gangbar.

Álvarez-Díaz
& Villalón

"BOUTIQUE HOTEL" APARTMENT, SAN JUAN, PUERTO RICO

A jet-setting doctor and his wife wanted their second home to have the panache of a boutique hotel, with extraordinary details that reflected their glitzy personalities. The timeline? As long as it took for partners Ricardo Álvarez-Díaz and Cristina Villalón to get the job done right.

The island location and the fact that most items were custom made or special ordered complicated matters, particularly with timing. When the handmade mosaic mural arrived from Italy—after a four-month wait—in a vertical instead of horizontal format, the whole job had to begin again, tacking on another four months. But such setbacks were taken in stride, in pursuit of the client's vision.

The layout was planned with entertaining in mind. The designers eliminated an existing loo to expand the family room and install a wet bar. Channeling a hotel lobby, the main living salon hosts numerous seating areas, including a banquette and outsize poufs. And in lieu of a traditional dining area, the designers envisioned a custom pub-style table with slipcovered stools.

Rich textures, assertive artwork, and unconventional lighting choices and wall coverings combine to create a setting that radiates pleasure. The dramatic palette contributes to a sense of exotic naughtiness, with its hints of opium den and Turkish harem. It's certainly not for the timid; the client, however, declared the project an overwhelming success.

From top: In the family room, as throughout much of the apartment, the walls were painted black to allow the abundant colors, textures, and patterns—of fabric and art—to bask in the limelight. At the far end of the room, a glass-tile wet bar and come-hither artwork set a smoky, night-clubby mood. ➘

2,350 sf
$380 per sf
Completed in 2 years

"The clients wanted their home to be original and spectacular! They love to entertain and wanted nothing of the status quo"

—CRISTINA VILLALÓN

Clockwise from opposite top: In the salon/dining room, a feature wall upholstered in an Osborne & Little botanical cushions the plush banquette; ottoman seating lends a hotel lobby vibe. The guest bathroom with lacquered vanity. The formerly open kitchen was enclosed to enlarge the adjacent salon; the System 30 cabinetry is by SCIC. In another corner of the salon, the shape and size of the light fixture echoes the curvaceous chaise longue below. The Boa chandelier crowning the dining table performs double duty as an art installation. ➤

1 ENTRY

2 SALON/DINING ROOM

3 KITCHEN

4 FAMILY ROOM

5 LAUNDRY ROOM

6 GUEST BEDROOM

7 MASTER SUITE

0 5 10   20

Clockwise from above: The glass walls of the master-bath shower, tucked in the corner between an extra-long sink and tub, help it recede into the background; large-format porcelain tiles confer a mural-like effect. Two daybeds make the second bedroom especially versatile. Fanciful table lamps stand at each end of the lowboy. ➴

Clockwise from near right: The powder room, with a distinctive Jaime Hayon sink-and-lamp design, is a study in black and gold. A mosaic mural by Sicis incorporates gold-leaf glass tesserae. The bold handpainted mural beside the diamond-tufted Fendi bed extends onto the ceiling; the pendant is by Baccarat. The gallerylike hallway, flanked with vibrant paintings and aglow with chandeliers, gets a serious grounding from a subdued Ligne Roset rug.

PROJECT TEAM ARCHITECTURE: RICARDO ÁLVAREZ-DÍAZ, INTERIOR DESIGN: CRISTINA VILLALÓN, PROJECT TEAM: CARENE PÉREZ ARÓSTEGUI, JOAQUIN HERNANDEZ
PHOTOGRAPHY CARLOS PÉREZ LÓPEZ/CHROMATICA GROUP

www.alvarezdiazvillalon.com

Morgante-Wilson Architects

LAKESIDE VILLA, CHICAGO'S NORTH SHORE

Clockwise from top left: Mahogany paneling and a coffered ceiling give the library an old-world ambience. Gray-washed antique oak beams—set off by pale fabrics and floor coverings—articulate the structure of the lake room, a family hangout space. A series of Venetian-plaster arches line the main corridor, which extends from the foyer to the family room. ➤

This intrepid family, avid travelers who'd spent several summers touring Italy, were inspired to build their own villa. The setting would not be on the Amalfi Coast, though; it would be on the shores of Lake Michigan. But how to tailor classical Italian elements to a modern lifestyle? Architects Elissa Morgante and Frederick Wilson took the project's reins and accomplished just that.

Carefully chosen materials and finishes set the tone. Terracotta floors and Venetian-plaster walls form a refined backdrop for European antiques and a selection of contemporary pieces. Details like aged-brick vaulting in the dining room, a zinc range hood, and the master bath's lively mosaic floor confer timelessness.

The couple specified that no spaces be off-limits to their young brood of three; for example, the casual yet elegant lake room is where the kids do homework and the clan gathers to enjoy the Wii. Family jam sessions—as well as piano lessons and concerts—occur in the music room, which substitutes for a formal living area. Less structured activities take place in the family room, whose deep L-shape sectional offers ample space for stretching out. Intimate seating arrangements in the more adultcentric, wood-paneled library invite chess players to partake.

To maximize the transporting views, the masterminds chose a mélange of neutrals for the palette. There's nothing to interfere with the vistas of water and foliage beyond—and no need at all to conjure the Italian coast.

"After several summers traveling the Italian countryside, this family decided it was high time to build their own villa—at home" —ELISSA MORGANTE AND FREDERICK WILSON

Clockwise from top:
The library offers
multiple seating
options for gaming
or reading; the
chandelier is from
Niermann Weeks.
The double-height
circular entry foyer
has a terracotta-tile
floor. Limestone walls,
a vaulted ceiling of
aged brick, antique
chandeliers, and a
mix of upholstered
chairs animate
the dining room.
The family room has
a contemporary
feel—and wrap-
around windows. ➥

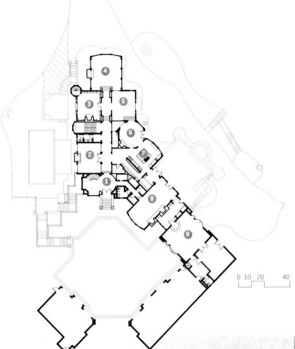

25,000 sf
6 bedrooms, 7 bathrooms,
3 half bathrooms

1 ENTRY FOYER

2 MUSIC ROOM

3 LIBRARY

4 FAMILY ROOM

5 LAKE ROOM

6 BREAKFAST ROOM

7 KITCHEN

8 DINING ROOM

9 BASEMENT LOUNGE

0 10 20 40

PROJECT TEAM FREDERICK WILSON, AIA, ELISSA MORGANTE, AIA, JOHN LEONARD, RENATA BUENROSTRO, K TYLER, DIANA ORTIZ
GENERAL CONTRACTOR TIMM T. MARTIN COMPANY
LANDSCAPE ARCHITECTURE CHALET LANDSCAPE, NURSERY & GARDEN CENTER
PHOTOGRAPHY MICHAEL ROBINSON

www.morgantewilson.com

Clockwise from top: The eclectic assemblage of music-room furnishings includes a Louis XV–style corner chair by Holly Hunt and a high-back wing chair from Ironies. The open-plan master bath features a detailed mosaic tile floor and a soaking tub with a view. A sitting area outside the powder room. The master bedroom is dressed in restful tones. The master suite's sitting room, with a tête-à-tête lounge and a meditation area, offers a haven at the start or end of day.

ANDREW R. ABRECHT
www.abrechtphoto.com

SEAN AIRHART
206-883-7435

ANTHONY BIANCIELLA
www.anthonybphotos.com

ANTOINE BOOTZ
www.antoinebootz.com

ANDREA BRIZZI
www.andreabrizzi.com

ROB BROWN
www.robbrownphoto.com

TODD BUCHANAN
www.toddbuchanan.com

BENNY CHAN / FOTOWORKS
www.fotoworks.cc

CHUCK CHOI
www.chuckchoi.com

MARK CRAEMER
www.markcraemer.com

JENNIFER FIORE
www.jenniferfiore.com

SCOTT FRANCES / OTTO
www.ottoarchive.com

ART GRAY
www.artgrayphotography.com

JILL GREER
www.greerphoto.com

KEN HAYDEN
www.kenhayden.com

MING-YI HSU
my1023@gmail.com

JAIME JUSTINIANI
jaimejustiniani@gmail.com

NATHAN KIRKMAN
www.nathankirkman.com

ANDREAS KORNFELD
www.andreaskornfeld.com

ERIC LAIGNEL
www.ericlaignel.com

PAMELA MASTERS
www.pamelamastersphotography.com

DAVID MATHESON
www.davidmathesonphotography.com

FAUSTO MAZZA
www.faustomazza.it

MCA ESTUDIO
www.mcaestudio.com.br

RACHEL McGINN
www.rachelmcginnphotography.com

JOSHUA McHUGH
www.joshuamchugh.com

KARYN MILLET
www.karynmillet.com

MATTHEW MILLMAN
www.matthewmillman.com

KEVIN J. MIYAZAKI
www.kevinmiyazaki.com

NACASA & PARTNERS
www.nacasa.co.jp

photographers index

PETER PAIGE
www.peterpaige.com

CARLOS PÉREZ LÓPEZ / CHROMATICA GROUP
www.chromaticagroup.com

TOM POWEL IMAGING
www.tompowelimaging.com

BEN RAHN / A-FRAME
www.aframestudio.ca

VAL RIOLO
www.valriolo.com

MICHAEL ROBINSON
www.mrobinsonphoto.com

LISA ROMEREIN
www.lisaromerein.com

GARRETT ROWLAND
www.garrettrowland.com

JUAN FELIPE RUBIO / EFEUNODOS
www.efeunodos.com

ANNIE SCHLECHTER
www.annieschlechter.com

JASON SCHMIDT
www.jasonschmidtartists.com

TRICIA SHAY
www.shayphoto.com

TOM SIBLEY
www.tomsibley.com

STUART SIEGEL
www.stusiegel.net

TODD A. SMITH
www.tasphoto.com

TONY SOLURI
www.soluriphotography.com

MELANIE SUGGS
706-264-7661

ALBERT VECERKA / ESTO
www.esto.com

PAUL WARCHOL
www.warcholphotography.com

SIMON WATSON
www.simonwatson.com

INTERIOR DESIGN®

editor in chief Cindy Allen

EXECUTIVE EDITOR
Elena Kornbluth

DEPUTY EDITOR
Edie Cohen (West/Southwest)

ARTICLES EDITOR
Annie Block

SENIOR EDITORS
Mark McMenamin
Deborah Wilk

MANAGING EDITOR
Helene E. Oberman

EDITORIAL ASSISTANT
Matthew Powell

DESIGNERS
Zigeng Li
Karla Lima

ASSISTANT TO THE EDITOR IN CHIEF
Athena Waligore

BOOKS EDITOR
Stanley Abercrombie

EDITOR AT LARGE
Craig Kellogg

CONTRIBUTING EDITORS
Raul Barreneche
Aric Chen
Laura Fisher Kaiser
Nicholas Tamarin
Peter Webster
Larry Weinberg

PRODUCTION MANAGER
Sarah Dentry / 646-805-0236 / sdentry@interiordesign.net

PREPRESS IMAGING SPECIALIST
Igor Tsiperson

RESEARCH DIRECTOR
Wing Leung / 646-805-0250

REPRINTS
Ness Feliciano / 708-660-8612 / fax 708-660-8613

INTERIORDESIGN.NET
ASSOCIATE WEB EDITOR
Meghan Edwards

ASSISTANT WEB EDITOR
Olivia Farquharson

ASSISTANT RESEARCH EDITOR
Ava Burke

DESIGNWIRE DAILY CONTRIBUTORS
Jesse Dorris
Sara Pepitone
Andrew Stone
Ian Volner

SANDOW®
Brands Powered by Innovation™

chairman and ceo of sandow media Adam I. Sandow

CHIEF FINANCIAL OFFICER AND CHIEF OPERATING OFFICER
Chris Fabian

VICE PRESIDENT, CREATIVE AND EDITORIAL
Yolanda E. Yoh

VICE PRESIDENT, WEB TECHNOLOGY
Christopher J. Coleman

EXECUTIVE VICE PRESIDENT, INFORMATION TECHNOLOGY
Juan Lopez

president Mark Strauss, hon. iida

ASSOCIATE PUBLISHER
Carol Cisco

DIGITAL MEDIA DIRECTOR
Pamela McNally

STRATEGIC AD DIRECTOR, NEW YORK
Gayle Shand

MARKETING DIRECTOR
Tina Brennan

EVENTS DIRECTOR
Rachel Long

ASSISTANT TO THE PRESIDENT
Kalyca Rei Murph

MARKETING
ART DIRECTOR
Denise Figueroa

SENIOR DESIGNER
Selena Chen

SENIOR MANAGER
Yasmin Spiro

COORDINATOR
Andrea Rosen / 646-805-0277

INTERIORDESIGN.NET
ASSISTANT WEB PRODUCER
Ashley Teater

SERVICES
BOOK SERIES DIRECTOR
Kathy Harrigan / 646-805-0243

HALL OF FAME DIRECTOR
Regina Freedman / 646-805-0270

CONTRACTS COORDINATOR
Sandy Campomanes / 646-805-0403

SPECIAL PROJECTS MANAGER
Kay Kojima / 646-805-0276

SALES
INTEGRATED MEDIA SALES
Karen Donaghy / 646-805-0291

SALES REPRESENTATIVE
Gina SanGiovanni-Ristic / 646-805-0283

INSIDE SALES DIRECTOR
Jonathan Kessler / 646-805-0279

SALES ASSOCIATE
Xiang Ping Zhu / 646-805-0269

SENIOR SALES COORDINATOR
Valentin Ortolaza / 646-805-0268

SALES ASSISTANT
Alana Taylor / 646-805-0271

PHILADELPHIA
Greg Kammerer / 610-738-7011 / fax 610-738-7195

ATLANTA, BUYERS GUIDE, E-SALES MANAGER
Craig Malcolm / 770-712-9245 / fax 770-234-5847

CHICAGO
Tim Kedzuch / 847-907-4050 / fax 847-556-6513
Julie McCarthy / 847-615-2077 / fax 847-713-4897

LOS ANGELES
Reed Fry / 949-223-1088 / fax 949-223-1089

FRANCE/GERMANY/POLAND
Mirek Kraczkowski / kraczko@aol.com / 48-22-401-7001 / fax 48-22-401-7016

ITALY
Riccardo Laureri / media@laureriassociates.it / 39-02-236-2500 / fax 39-02-236-4411

ASIA
Quentin Chan / quentinchan@leadingm.com / 852-2366-1106 / fax 852-2366-1107

AUDIENCE MARKETING
SENIOR DIRECTOR
Katharine Tucker